What others have said about Geoffrey's stop smoking programme…

I stopped smoking with Geoffrey five years ago and stopped alcohol two years ago. I cannot begin to explain just how wonderful the whole experience has been. I feel free and completely me without poisoning myself… I am in charge of my life again. Thank you.
Cristina

As one of nature's natural sceptics I couldn't see how just reading a book would stop me smoking. I read Geoffrey's book (so that my friend who stopped with Geoffrey would leave me in peace) and he made it so easy. I smell so much better, and my wife is delighted that I've stopped snoring. Any one who doesn't stop smoking with Geoffrey must be mad!
David

Never believed that I could do it, From forty a day to zero without the slightest problem. I feel great I've even started running. Brilliant! Thanks
Philip

It's a year and a half since I stopped smoking thanks to a session I went to in Madrid. The truth is that at first I thought it would be difficult as I had tried to stop many times and it was impossible for me to manage more than one day without smoking. Until a friend told me about the sessions and I decided to try it out. And I must say it was the best thing I could have done as I went out directly without smoking and the next days went by without me needing to put a cigarette in my mouth and the best of all is that the withdrawal was hardly noticeable — like the pinch of a little child. I recommend it to everyone who wants to stop smoking. If you think you can't, try it. It's worth it. *Miguel*

Hi Geoffrey, hi Rhea. Thanks for the wonderful work that you people do. I must tell you that the 16th of April is a day that I will never forget for as long as I live. It was the day that I got back my life. It was the day that at last I managed to clear my head of all those strange ideas and above all the fears that tormented me. I smoked more than two packs a day and even though I did stop smoking with you before, I stupidly took

one puff and I started again. Looking back I can see that I felt incapable of stopping. I didn't feel strong enough although I wanted to stop smoking, above all for my kids who I want to see grow up, and want for them a healthy dad and none of the suffering that losing someone as result of that shit (tobacco) must bring. Now that finally I've done it (stopped smoking), I am so happy. My body has experienced such surprising wonderful changes. I don't get tired like before. I don't have that disgusting cough, I breath perfectly, I go upstairs easily, my breath doesn't stink of tobacco, neither does my hair, clothes or skin the most marvelous thing is when I kiss my sons and they don't say "Eurghh…you smell bad". Sadly I have seen friends and family killed by this shit (tobacco). I don't ever want to suffer that same fate. By stopping smoking I have taken an important first step to make sure that this. doesn't happen. I will be forever grateful. Than you for giving me this new life. I am sincerely grateful.
Kike

Hi Geoffrey, I just want to say that three months ago I came to your stop smoking course and thanks to you guys I stopped smoking. I no longer live chained to this absurd addiction that had me hooked for half my life. I am now 44 years old, I started smoking when I was just 13 or even a bit younger, I got to where I was smoking two packs a day. I was one of those smokers who felt that I couldn't stop smoking but you got me to see that I could and I did. I would recommend that anyone who wants to stop smoking attend this course because what has worked for can work for you too.
Raul

Hi Geoffrey, hi Rhea. This is Almudena from Bilbao. Just one word: Thank you.

Hello, This is Carlos. The nicotine withdrawal is over and I feel better every day. I think about smoking every now and then but it's just a second. I look at my new wathch and the moment passes. Greetings.

Hi. I started smoking when I was fifteen. I am now sixty-four and had tried to stop on many occasions but with no success. I came to your course four months ago and this time I am convinced that I have become an ex-smoker and I feel very happy about this. I send you this email in thanks to the great help your therapy meant to me to manage to conquer this awful addiction. Hoping that this will help others. With best wishes, *Santiago.*

Hi, this is Beatriz from Valencia. On the 20 of November 2010 I went to one of Geoffrey's sessions and have not smoked since then. Thank you. After two months free I can truly see now that nicotine does create dependence but that one can free oneself from it. Of all the times that I have stopped smoking, this is it... I truly believe it as I have not had to focus so much in will-power, rather convince myself WITHOUT FEAR. *Beatriz*

Dear Geoffrey, Rhea... I'm getting in touch with you again, having stopped smoking for good quite a few weeks ago now (since the 17th of February). Since then, apart from not putting on any weight I've allowed myself a variety of enjoyable experiences which I would have had difficulty in enjoying before whilst I was tied to tobacco. Amongst these experiences I have been able to travel abroad without the need to have cigarettes to hand. I spent four days in Brussels (two working, two for pleasure) and at no time did I feel the need to depend on the "chimney". Not only that, I visited all the most important buildings in Brussels without tiring. In the past, when I was a smoker it would have cost me rather more effort and I wouldn't have managed walking the whole day. I also took a pleasure trip to Berlin and that's where I really realized how beautiful it is to enjoy life without the need for tobacco – bearing in mind the fact that the Berliners smoke a lot and drink even more. I reckon that each day I walked about 10 kilometres with no effort whatsoever, including crossing the Tiergarten from the Zoo to the museum island. I noticed the greatest improvement in my third pleasure trip to Extremadura, in the Jerte Valley – an idyllic landscape where I dared to walk the "Ruta de la Garganta de los Infiernos" (Route of the throat of hells). What was incredible is that I managed all the ups and downs with relatively little effort and had no problem in finishing it in 7 hours. Once again, I thank you for this book. It helped me greatly to reinforce the concepts of Carr's book. I was reminded of you during a work dinner in Brussels when we were given mango as dessert – something I had never tried... Many thanks. *Fran Ruiz*

For more comments: www.esfacilsisabescomo.es

I dedicate this book to my children: Claudine, Erika, Kiira, Xavier, Ishtar and my granddaughter Amaya.

Why Did You Start Smoking Again?

Find out, end the drama and get on with your life

Geoffrey Molloy

Why Did You Start Smoking Again?
Find out, end the drama and get on with your life

Wide Awake Life Maps ©

Why did you start smoking again?
Author Geoffrey Molloy

Cover design: María Amat Artigas

Wide Awake Life Maps
Es fácil… ¡si sabes cómo! S.L
Finca Las Bardas
39408 Cóo, Los Corrales de Buelna
Cantabria (Spain)
http://www.wideawakelifemaps.com
http://www.esfacilsisabescomo.es

Series: Wide Awake Life Maps
ISBN-13: 978-1466304468
ISBN-10: 1466304464

Every effort has been made to ensure that the information in this book is accurate. The information in this book will be relevant to the majority of people but may not be applicable in each individual case so it is advised that professional medical advice is obtained for specific information on personal health matters. Neither the publisher nor the author accepts any legal responsibility for any personal injury or other damage or loss arising from the use or misuse of the information and advice in this book.

Printed in USA

Acknowledgements

My thanks to Rhea, my wife, business partner and the many clients with whom it has been my great privilege to work with. I salute your courage. You have also been my greatest teachers. My thanks too to Mireya Ceballos and the constant cheerfulness she brings to her work with us.

CONTENTS

Foreword

If you are reading this foreword then you are probably a smoker asking yourself, "Is this book for me?" or perhaps you are thinking of this book for a loved one.

My name is Geoffrey Molloy. I stopped smoking eighteen years ago. I have been a non-smoker since that time. My wife, Rhea and I have spent the past sixteen years helping many thousands of people to stop smoking. Together we brought Allen Carr's Easyway to Stop smoking to Spain in 1995. Allen's book has been a great success. However, a comment we hear frequently is, "I stopped smoking with Allen Carr's book and I was a happy non-smoker. Then stupidly, I became over confident and felt that I could get away with smoking just one cigarette. Well, here I am smoking the same or even more than before! I feel angry with myself and so frustrated. I re-read the book but it doesn't seem to help. I'm desperate. What can I do?" *This book has been written with you in mind.*

Even if you have never read any stop smoking book in your life; even if you believe yourself to be an impossible case, if you read this book with an open mind and follow the instructions, you will not only stop smoking quickly and painlessly but you will also feel delighted and free as a non-smoker. You won't miss smoking or feel that you have lost anything. If you have already stopped smoking but don't feel happy as a non-smoker, read this book and follow the instructions to free yourself completely.

Do not believe in anything simply because you have heard it. Do not believe in anything simply because it is spoken and rumoured by many. Do not believe in anything because it is found written in your religious books. Do not believe in anything merely on the authority of your teachers and elders. Do not believe in traditions because they have been handed down for many generations. But after observation and analysis, when you find anything that agrees with reason and is conducive to the good and benefit of one and all, then accept it and live up to it.

Siddhartha Gautama

Introduction

In 1993 I stopped smoking with Allen Carr's Easy to Stop Smoking. For that I feel grateful to this day. I wrote a letter to thank Allen and invite him to lunch in Marbella where I lived with my wife and family. Shortly afterwards we enjoyed the first of several meals together. It was during one of these meals that the idea of bringing his programme to Spain was raised. Subsequently, in 1995 Rhea and I translated his book and set out to get it published in Spain. It was an uphill struggle. We had little money and five young children. Allen and his 'Easyway to Stop Smoking' were hardly known outside of the UK at that time and not at all in Spain. Two earlier Spanish translations of his book had failed and sunk without trace. Rhea and I set to work. Once we completed the translation we put a great deal of effort into finding a publisher. In the meantime we devoted ourselves to adapting the live session to Spanish culture. In October 1995 we started to give our first sessions.

Using my own life experience together with the experience gained working with freeing smokers, I began to work with other addictions and wellbeing in general. I have also written a book which will enable anyone to live happily without alcohol.

During the past sixteen years Rhea and I have helped many thousands of people to stop smoking. There is no other company or person in Spain with as much direct successful experience as we have of liberating people from their addiction to nicotine. The e-mails, letters and messages we receive from people who have stopped smoking with us transmit a great sense of joy, relief and satisfaction. Yet in spite of the immense sense of liberation and the marvellous increase in energy, health and self-esteem they feel when they become non-smokers, some, often for the most absurd of reasons, become hooked again.

This book has been written in order to enable any smoker who wants to stop smoking to do so, quickly, painlessly and to live the rest of his life, delighted with his decision. I have thought especially of those who managed to stop smoking, but started again. However, even if you believe that you have never tried to stop smoking, or have tried but never lasted more than five minutes; or if you have stopped smoking but are not happy about it, then this book is for you.

My promise to you is the following: this book will enable you to stop smoking easily, without suffering and enjoy life as a non-smoker, not just the same, but more than you did as a smoker. More importantly you will also be able *to stop stopping smoking*. That might seem a strange thing to mark as an objective but for a large part of my life as a smoker, stopping smoking was always hanging over me. I was always going to stop smoking 'soon'; negotiating, rationalising, trying to smoke less, stopping at night, saying as I went to bed, "Right that's it, I've stopped," and the following morning lighting my first cigarette with a sense of self-loathing and resignation. The price of living like that was my vitality, my physical, mental and spiritual wellbeing.

It was only once I had stopped smoking that I realized just how negatively smoking had affected every aspect of my life. When I did stop, it was such a relief, not just to stop smoking but to finally *stop stopping smoking*. That is what this book is about: to set you free definitively from your addiction to nicotine. Once you have read this book, you will understand why people become addicted to nicotine and the ways in which many factors and players have combined and in some cases conspired to ingrain smoking and many other kinds of addiction deeply into our culture.

Stopping smoking is easy. You might find that difficult to believe right now, but ask yourself, "Why shouldn't it be easy?" All you have to do is put out one cigarette and not light another. Remember first of all that smoking isn't something that *happens* to you. *You* light the cigarette. *You* smoke it. No one forces *you* to do it. That is excellent news! For if it is you that lights the cigarette, then the power to stop and free yourself must also lie in your hands. Stopping smoking is really easy if you know how; but to understand the *how* you have to understand the *why* and to understand why you must first know where to put your attention.

When you smoke, you purposely and systematically introduce a range of toxic chemicals into your body. One of the reasons why governments and the medical profession have such an abysmal record for helping smokers stop smoking is their mistaken but very profitable belief (profitable for the pharmaceutical industry and their helpers) that you can stop smoking by putting even more toxic chemicals into your body. This, in spite of the mass of *independent evidence* which shows that medication and cigarette substitutes are ineffective and sometimes lethal. (See references 1 and 2 in the section at the end of the book.) This is because doctors (and smokers) tend to focus on the reasons for which we shouldn't smoke, not why we do smoke. In other words their attention is in the wrong place.

Why did you start smoking again?

Our attention is drawn naturally to movement in the foreground. It is how we have evolved. This means that most people, including doctors, tend to focus on the symptoms of the diseases caused by smoking. However well your doctor might understand the horrific consequences of smoking, it doesn't help either you or him to understand *why* a smoker smokes. This is an important distinction: foreground or background. For example, when we talk about making a good cup of tea we tend to focus on the quality of the tea and not on the quality of the water with which we make the drink. However, the quality of the water is every bit as important.

Thanks to modern medicine we have eliminated much unnecessary suffering with diseases like rubella, scarlet fever, smallpox, TB, polio. However, the pharmaceutical approach which has been successful with these diseases is ineffective for other conditions and may even be dangerous. This is an example of the syndrome coined by Abraham Maslow: 'When the only tool you have is a hammer, you tend to see all of your problems as nails'.

More than half of the diseases that we suffer in this modern age are self-inflicted. A recent report in the Journal of the American Medical Association (JAMA) found that the fourth highest cause of death in the USA is from pharmacological side effects of *correctly* used medication (that is to say used exactly as directed) and does not include accidents. (Ref. 3.). In many countries smoking is the number one self-inflicted disease in terms both of sheer number of deaths (about five million a year) and the horrific reduction in quality of life.

Many diseases exist and persist in our society because of our tendency to ignore the causes (background) and our focus on treating the symptoms (foreground). For example, it is widely recognized that the principal causes of heart disease are bad diet and a sedentary lifestyle. This is exacerbated by the food industry's brainwashing to get us to buy and eat stuff laden with fat, salt and sugar by providing misleading information about the ingredients and exaggerating the health benefits. The consequence of diets based on such 'foods' is deteriorating health and wellbeing. The solutions offered by the health industry do not treat these causes. Instead, we have expensive and unnecessary surgery such as the gastric balloon, multiple bypass operations, diabetes II medication, anti-cholesterol medication, hypertensive medication – to name a few. All of these treatments, whilst profitable for many pharmaceutical and food companies, treat the symptoms and not the causes.

Both musicians and professional speakers understand the importance of not only words or sounds but also the space between

17

them. Without the space between the notes there cannot be music. It is easy to become so fixated on the sounds and words that we sometimes forget to pay attention to the space between the sounds and words, which can be of equal or greater importance. A smoker is so fixated on the 'pleasure' of smoking a cigarette that he does not see the constant background suffering he endures just to experience a momentary relief when he lights up. This isn't helped by the fact that most smokers have been smoking since adolescence and do not know what adult life is like without smoking. They have no other experience.

Never lose sight of the fact that the tobacco industry has one single objective: to make money. If you have to die or suffer horrific debilitating disease for them to do that, well they won't mind a bit. In order to do this they have to get children hooked and keep adults hooked. They are aided and abetted in this by the corruption, apathy and self-interest of many industries, associations, government bodies and professions which we believe mistakenly have our interests at heart. They don't! The fact is that the priority of most of these bodies is to protect their own interests and those of the industries which directly or indirectly fund them. Most people grossly underestimate the power of big industry to shape the way we think, distort legislative process and corrupt the institutions in which we place our trust.

The only way to free ourselves from nicotine addiction (smoking) is to wake up and liberate ourselves of the tobacco and PR industry's manipulation of our mental maps and models (perceptions) and to see things as they really are. Only then can we take appropriate action to free ourselves.

At no time in this book will I try to frighten you into stopping smoking. It doesn't work. In fact fear usually provokes the opposite effect. Think, one of the moments in which a smoker lights a cigarette is when she feels frightened or nervous. Frighten a smoker and the first thing she will do is look for a cigarette. However, if you do want to know what the WHO has said about tobacco please look at Reference 4 in the section at the end of this book.

Stopping smoking is marvellous. You will not only feel as good as you did when you were a smoker but much, much better. You might think I'm talking about the health and economic benefits which are tremendous, but the best benefits are mental and spiritual. It is an immense relief not to have every aspect of your life conditioned by a smelly, disgusting, anti-social and deadly addiction. The freedom of not having to smoke is simply marvellous.

Why did you start smoking again?

The fact is that there are absolutely no genuine benefits to smoking. *Not a single one!* When you stop smoking you lose nothing and you give up nothing. Stopping and staying stopped is not only easy but also a real relief.

So the questions are: why then do we start in the first place and why do some smokers stop smoking, feel free and delighted not to smoke and then start again? In this book you will find the answers to these questions. You will also find all of the information you need, not just to stop smoking but in the words of a client: "to stop stopping smoking".

Geoffrey Molloy

1

How to get the most out of this book

We can't solve problems by using the same kind of thinking we used when we created them. **Einstein**.

Practically all of the people who attend our sessions do so by recommendation. They know a friend, a neighbour or a family member — an 'impossible case', someone who had tried 'everything' to stop smoking, who after one of our sessions not only stopped smoking but was obviously delighted; they did not suffer — in fact the very opposite — they were euphoric about not having to smoke. Most smokers come to the session full of a mixture hope, fear and doubt. Most do not have much faith in their ability to stop smoking. Perhaps like you, they have tried to stop and failed, perhaps many times. Many have come to the conclusion that there is perhaps some sort of weakness within them, that they are a difficult case, that perhaps they have 'addictive genes', or they secretly suspect they might lack moral fibre, willpower or have some hidden desire for self-harm.

Things appear more difficult than they are because most smokers have usually been smoking for so long that they cannot remember what life feels like as a non-smoker. By this I do not mean that the longer you smoke the harder it is to stop. It isn't. (In fact the number of years that you've been a smoker is irrelevant.) Nearly all of us start smoking when we are no more than children. I, for example, smoked my first cigarette when I was only ten years old. When I stopped smoking twenty-five years later, I had no experience of life as an adult or adolescent non-smoker. For most smokers being a non-smoking adult is something that falls outside of their experience. My life as a smoker was all that I knew. The cough, the constant nicotine craving, the reduced vitality were normal for me, as was constantly having to make sure that I always had tobacco to hand, planning my life according to the next predicted opportunity to smoke. The fear of stopping smoking and the fear of carrying on smoking had always been a part of my life and because of that had become almost invisible to me. I include here a Taoist story which sums it up rather well:

A long time ago in a remote valley, there lived a farmer. One day, whilst walking in the mountains, he found an eagle's nest with a single egg. He carefully picked it up and stowed it in his pack. As evening fell he made his way back home to his farm. When he got home he put the egg in with the few chickens he kept in his chicken-run. The mother hen was the proudest chicken you could possibly imagine, chest puffed out with pride, sitting atop this magnificent egg. She incubated that egg with great care. Sure enough, some weeks later, a fine, healthy egret emerged from the egg.

So it was that the eagle grew up with its brother and sister chicks. It learned to do all the things chickens do. It clucked, scratched and pecked in the dirt for insects and worms. By flapping its wings furiously, it could even fly just a few feet in the air before crashing down to earth in a shower of dust and feathers. It believed absolutely that it was a chicken. *It had never known anything else.*

The years past and one day the eagle-who-thought-he-was-a-chicken happened to look up at the sky. High overhead, soaring majestically and effortlessly with scarcely a single beat of its great powerful golden wings, was an eagle! "Wow! What's that?" cried the now aged eagle-who-thought-he-was-a-chicken in awe. "It's magnificent, glorious! So much power and grace! It's beautiful!" "That's an eagle," replied a nearby chicken. "That's the King of the Birds. It's free. It's a bird of the air... not like us. We're only chickens. We are only birds of the earth." With that they all cast their eyes downwards once more and continued clucking, scratching and digging in the dirt. Thus the eagle lived and died a chicken... *because that's all it believed itself to be.*

Whilst we smoke we are in many ways like the eagle who believed he was a chicken. The eagle didn't have defective genes or a 'chicken' personality; *he just didn't know any different.* In much the same way a smoker doesn't smoke because he has 'smoker's genes' or a 'smoker's personality'. *He simply knows no other life.*

What makes this analogy so appropriate is that the quality of life of a smoker is like that of the chicken: scratching around, trapped in a rather depressing, confined existence. Stop smoking and you become free like the eagle, so much more powerful in every way. You at least get a chance to realize your full potential, something you cannot do as a smoker.

The most important difference between the smoker and the eagle-who-thought-he-was-a-chicken is that we humans are (usually) more intelligent than chickens.

After we realize that we have been conned into the great nicotine scam (after all none of us decided to become smokers) and that we are hooked, we start to look for a way out.

Because we usually have little or no experience of life as an adult non-smoker, stopping smoking feels like a step into the unknown. Many organizations, industries and politicians are happy to mislead and exploit the smoker for their own benefit. I quote the 'Golden Rule':

'He who has the gold makes the rules'.

Most of the officially approved information about stopping smoking is thinly veiled marketing for largely ineffective medication and cigarette substitutes.

Perhaps the most insidious aspect of this is how, at the end of the day, everyone blames and chastises the smoker. They forget that the smoker wants to free himself. Smokers are nagged, bullied, pressured, despised, stigmatized and humiliated at every turn. But it is the smoker himself who wants more than anyone else to be free of his slavery to nicotine. The smoker would stop smoking quickly and easily if only he could get some accurate, useful information. Smokers do not smoke because they are sick, stupid or defective in some way; it is just that they (and society as a whole) are deliberately misinformed or perhaps it would be better to say lied to. They were lied to when they started and lied to when they try to stop.

Imagine for a moment that you find yourself for the first time in a foreign city. Let's call it Gotham. You are on a vital mission and you have to find a certain place there. You are lost but not too worried; in fact you feel pretty laid-back because you have an official map which you bought from a government-approved map-seller and you are confident that with this map you can complete your mission. You start out confidently, but it seems that no matter how closely you follow the map, you remain lost. Still, you feel that it cannot be that difficult, but try as you might, you just cannot find that place. After months of trying, you get bored and decide to leave it for a while – maybe it will be easier to find later.

Years go by and you come to realize that this mission is much more important than you thought. In fact it might even be a matter of life and death. You get out your map and study it closely. *(What you don't know is that, although the map has the title 'City map of Gotham', it has in fact been secretly and maliciously manipulated into a misleading jumble of many different maps, because the people of the city know that the longer you are delayed there, the more money you will spend there and the richer they and their friends will become.)* You are not too

23

stupid or too proud to seek out help so you ask people around you for directions. They confirm that the map is right and that 'everyone knows that!' However, try as you might, you remain lost. You go to see a person that they tell you can help. Although this person considers himself an expert in finding the place you are looking for, he is really only an expert in telling you what will happen to you if you don't find the place, describing the terrible consequences if you don't complete your mission. In fact, he feels that if he can scare you enough with stories about the unfortunate people who didn't make it, that he will somehow help. He also sells you these outrageously expensive pills. You try them. They make you feel nervous and sick. The expert tells you not to worry that the pills make you feel nervous and sick, just to take them anyway and they will help you find your way. This sounds odd to you, so you ask him how taking pills could possible help you find your way to a place. The expert starts to explain but you soon realize that he really doesn't know. You quickly get the feeling that he's just repeating something the pill manufacturer told him.

So now you feel nervous and sick, but you're still lost. You decide that maybe it's your attitude that is wrong so you work on making your attitude more positive. Now you have a smile on your face but you are still lost. You feel increasingly desperate. People blame you for your inability to find your way. They tell you that you have a 'gets-lost-easily personality', or some sort of genetic weakness. You have spent years trying to find your way; you can't and everyone, it seems, blames you.

Just when you are at the point of giving up, you meet someone who knows about the scam of the manipulated map. She gives you the correct map. Suddenly everything makes sense. You also feel relieved to discover that you don't have gets-lost-easily genes or personality. It wasn't you at all. It was just that ***the map they gave you was wrong.***

I tried many times to stop smoking and like everyone else who was using the wrong map, I always suffered the same symptoms: bad temper, irritability and sooner or later (usually sooner) I'd be smoking the same as I always had − two packs or more a day. The worst of it was that each time I failed I believed that that the problem was within me. Frequently I would light my first cigarette of the day with a sense of self-loathing, helplessness and depression.

I have spent the last sixteen years enabling smokers to see the reality, to free themselves. You too can stop smoking and free yourself for once and for all of the thrall of nicotine addiction. You just have to read this book, understand what is written, and follow some simple instructions.

Why did you start smoking again?

Instruction number one – Follow all of the instructions: The instructions below are based on years of experience with thousands of smokers. Every single one of them is there for a purpose. You are free to follow or not follow these instructions. By following all of them, you will not only stop smoking but also remain free forever. In our sessions people often ask, "So what type of smoker is successful with you?" The answer is: "The ones that follow the instructions". That is accurate. I have treated all types of people – male, female, young, old; people from all walks of life; from different racial groups; people with varying levels of education, from different social classes, with different types of personalities and genes. The successful ones all have the same thing in common: *They followed all of the instructions.* There are no frills or adornments in these instructions. Follow all of them and you will free yourself permanently and easily from nicotine addiction. If at any time you want to discuss the ideas in this book with someone, you are free to do so. However, a warning: If anyone should give you advice that contradicts or modifies the information or instructions in this book, *ignore their advice*. To be successful, you must follow all of the instructions in this book.

Instruction number two – Open your mind: Perhaps your first reaction is, "Well that's easy, I'm a very open-minded person." Please bear with me whilst I take you through what I mean by being open-minded. Firstly, I have yet to meet a person who would describe themselves as *closed*-minded. Most of us like to think of ourselves as fair and open-minded. That is to say, we first consider impartially all the facts and points of view and based upon that impartial consideration, we arrive at an opinion. Unfortunately, the mind works in exactly the opposite way. We already have an opinion about almost everything and we tend to use any information we receive to prove that the opinion we hold is the right one.

We navigate the world through mental maps. Our understanding and perceptions depend on these maps. The problem arises when we don't see our mental map or point of view for what it is: *just a map*, a sometimes useful point of view. We mistakenly believe that our point of view is *'Reality'* and we use whatever information we receive to prove that we're right. We behave like this even if our point of view works against us. *Remember: The map is just a map; it is not the territory*. I am not asking you for blind faith; be sceptical by all means, but not only with what you read here but especially with the ideas that you already hold about smoking. After all, it is those very ideas, that map, that keep you smoking.

There is a wonderful story which comes out of the Orient, known as 'Beginner's Mind'. It is about a great spiritual master and a student.

The student was himself a professor and had studied many books and teachings. Each time the master spoke of an idea, the student would

say, "Ah yes, I have heard of that," or "Yes, well that's very interesting, especially when compared to the theories of so-and-so" and so it went on. No matter what the teacher said, the student would display his knowledge by making an observation or comment. After a few hours the master stopped and offered some tea to the student. Whilst the master quietly served the tea, the student continued expounding his own points of view. The master poured the visitor's cup to the brim and then kept pouring. The student watched the overflowing cup until he could no longer restrain himself, blurting out, "It's overfull! No more will go in!" "You are like this cup," the master replied. "How can I teach you anything unless you first empty your cup?"

The moral of this story is that in the beginner's mind there are many possibilities, whilst in the mind of the expert, there are few. If you want to be successful, adopt the beginners mind.

Yes, but I'm a special or difficult case

A common belief that acts as a barrier to success is the 'special case' syndrome, the inflexible attitude of the smoker who believes, "I am a special case, I am unusual, I am a particularly difficult case." Within a short time of being in the session and listening to others, most clients realize that they suffer the same addiction as their fellow smokers. Essentially whilst we smoke, we are all the same. However, a minority don't want to let go of their special status. Some even seem quite proud of the fact that nothing works for them. Throughout the session they keep saying to themselves things like, "*I* am a special case," "What Geoffrey is saying might apply to the others but *I* am different," or "*I* am different from the others, therefore what Geoffrey says simply cannot apply to me." Thus, no matter what I say, they will use the information to confirm their existing point of view, without ever once realising that it is precisely this point of view that keeps them smoking.

Whilst I smoked I too was convinced that I was a particularly difficult case. I had tried many times to free myself and failed. I came to believe that I was an especially hopeless case. For example, if I woke up during the night I would usually smoke. I remember thinking, "God! Geoffrey, you're such a saddie, such an addict that you even wake up to smoke." Eighteen years without smoking and I still wake up during the night but without the need or desire to smoke. What is clear is that my waking up during the night had nothing to do with being a smoker. *However, whilst I believed myself to be a hopeless addict, I was convinced that my waking up at night was because of my smoking.*

Another barrier to opening your mind can be the defensive posture smokers often adopt as a necessary way of protecting themselves from others and to maintain self-respect. It goes like this: All smokers have tried to stop smoking at some time with the possible exception of those youngsters who have just started and still believe that they are not hooked. When I say that in the sessions, there is always someone who will shake their head and say, "Me, I've never tried to stop." Many smokers confuse an attempt to stop with the duration of the attempt. Most attempts to stop smoking don't last more than a few minutes or even seconds. Having failed, the smoker will often console himself by saying something like, "Well that wasn't a *serious* attempt." The most important consequence of this experience is that in his heart the smoker feels he cannot stop. This situation is made worse by the pressure all smokers feel to stop smoking: pressure from their spouse, their children, the workplace, their doctor, friends and from society in general. The smoker wants to stop, feels incapable of doing so and he also feels persecuted. The natural reaction to such a situation is to adopt a defensive posture, saying things such as, "I absolutely *love* smoking," "Well, you've got to die of something, right?" "Never trust a man without a vice," "Everything causes cancer nowadays." Sound familiar? Whilst this posture might have afforded you some emotional protection from family and rabid anti-smokers, to continue with this posture whilst you read this book simply acts as a barrier to understanding.

An aspect of this defensive posture is rationalisation. White lies are the lies we tell others to spare their feelings. Rationalisation is the lies we tell ourselves to spare our own feelings (to be able to get on with our lives). For example, the number of cigarettes a smoker will admit to smoking depends on who's doing the asking. We have the doctor/spouse figure: *"Rarely more than 10."* Then we have the figure we reserve for other smokers: *"twenty a day."* We also have the figure that we reserve for ourselves, a figure which we often keep deliberately vague. You know that you smoke more than a pack day but you don't really want to know how much more. Be aware of this tendency to self-delusion. The problem is that we end up believing our own lies. Be aware of the automatic, habitual answers and justifications that spring to mind as you are reading this book. However, if whilst reading, you experience a sense of resonance or a moment of insight, pause for a moment to reflect, allowing yourself to fully experience the flavour and ramifications of your insight.

Instruction number three – Don't dip: This is very important. Read the chapters in the order in which they are presented. Some people fall into the trap of believing that, because they are very busy or that they believe that they already understand most of what is written, they can save time by skimming, reading just the information they believe applies specifically to them. They start leafing through the book to find that part which they feel might be the most useful. This book does not work like that. Read the book in the order that it is presented. If you feel that you need to stop for a moment to re-read or to better understand something, do it. This book follows a logical process. Follow that process.

Instruction number four – Do not cut down, stop smoking or deliberately change your smoking routine until you finish this book: Keep smoking just as you always have until you reach the appropriate part of the book. This is simply to avoid unnecessary distractions. Imagine, if you had to read this book without smoking a cigarette, it would be difficult if not impossible for you to take in and assimilate anything. You will know when to stop smoking because it will be in the instructions. Up to that point don't stop or cut down. Simply smoke when you feel like it. Don't worry if you find that you are smoking more or less than usual; just go with the flow and smoke as you feel like it. The only exception to this rule is if you have already stopped smoking, then **DON'T START AGAIN.** It will work just fine for you too.

Instruction number five – Remember... your past is not your future!
It is fashionable nowadays to talk of a mythical figure, the 'hardcore smoker', who, according to simplistic and sensationalist press reporting, finds it difficult or impossible to stop because he has 'addict's genes'. There is no conclusive scientific evidence for the existence of such genes. The cause of most problems in life, is not your DNA, rather it is how you perceive yourself and the world in which you live. In other words what you believe.

Why did you start smoking again?

Let us take two smokers. One tries to stop smoking (by whatever means) and fails. He might feel bad for a moment but then starts to think things like, "Perhaps it wasn't the right moment," "Maybe I did something wrong," "Lots of other people stop smoking and seem happy about it," "It must be possible for me to stop smoking," "I've just got to find out what I did wrong and how to do it differently or better next time," "It's not personal, I'm no better or worse than any other smoker; I just got addicted like all those other smokers who are now non-smokers." His point of view is logical and based on evidence. Sooner or later he is likely to succeed.

Now let's look at another smoker who tries and fails. This smoker thinks, "I am a failure," "There is something wrong with me," "It's probably genetic; I will never get free," "I'm weak," "Hardly anyone really stops," "Anyway, everyone knows that once a smoker, always a smoker." Beliefs such as these become self-fulfilling prophecies. He will give up sooner. He may not even bother to try to stop. He will then take the failure as confirmation that his negative beliefs about himself are correct. What he cannot see is that it is the erroneous negative belief about himself that caused the problem and not the problem that caused the negative (and frankly) unhelpful belief.

It is an undeniable fact that millions of smokers, just like you, have stopped smoking and are content to be non-smokers. So if they can do it, logically it must be possible for you too. *Remember: your past is not your future.*

Instruction number six − Start with the right attitude: The very idea of stopping smoking can produce fear and even panic. This fear and panic is caused by misunderstanding the problem. It is caused by the cigarette. Non-smokers simply do not suffer these fears. Just remember that stopping smoking is wonderful. Nothing bad is happening when you read this book. See the positive side. Imagine how wonderful you will feel to be free of the bondage of nicotine addiction without the need or desire to smoke, to soar like an eagle. What you gain when you stop smoking is no less than your freedom. Freedom from the fear and drudgery of addiction. You get your life back. Allow yourself to feel positive about reading this book. Allow yourself to feel excited about what you can achieve by reading this book. This is an exciting step. Go at it with an open mind. Enjoy the experience.

You may have negative beliefs about your ability to stop smoking. As you read the foregoing chapter, you may have thought, "It's all very well you saying that but I know what I'm like; I know that I'm an impossible case." If, whilst reading this book, you find that your thinking is taking you down that negative path, stop and rally the evidence. Millions of other 'difficult' cases have stopped. In fact, everyone is a 'difficult' case, which means no one is. You are no different to any other smoker. When you and I lit that first experimental cigarette neither of us did so thinking that we would have to smoke all day, everyday, for the rest of our lives. No one starts smoking like that! Why should it be so difficult to stop smoking and be delighted about it? All you have to do is not light the next cigarette. Nobody forces you to smoke. Fortunately, it is you who lights the cigarette; it is something within your control. Millions of smokers have liberated themselves. Remember, they too felt hopeless and frightened about stopping smoking and they are now free. Anyone can stop smoking. I quote Mr Spock: "To believe otherwise is simply illogical."

Instruction number seven – Take responsibility: Until we take responsibility for something, we cannot change it. I mean how could we? Or why would we? After all it's not our responsibility, not our choice. Ask yourself the question, "Why do I want to stop smoking?" If your answer is something along the lines of, "I *have to* stop smoking, I don't have any choice," watch out! The very moment we say, "I *have to*", we renounce responsibility. To *have to* implies obligation, a lack of choice, doing something against your will. Until a smoker takes responsibility, he cannot be implicated in his own cure. It is almost like saying, "Look, *I don't want to* stop smoking *but I have to* because... my doctor told me to, my wife won't stop nagging me; for my children's health." All smokers, at some time, feel pressured to stop smoking. This, however, doesn't make them stop. If you are reading this book then do so because **you want to** not because **you have to**. This desire to stop smoking is no surprise because the most powerful drive is the desire to survive. Even if you don't realise that you are addicted, there is always a part of you that tells you that you're doing something stupid. As much or as creatively as we might try to rationalise our way out of it, the survival drive is strong and the feeling that we are doing something stupid remains.

Most clients who show up at a back-up session and have started smoking again express regret, feel that they made a mistake, want to understand what it was and how to put it right.

A minority of clients who attend our sessions will not, for whatever reason, take responsibility. They tend to describe their experience as if they were a passive bystander, as though things just happen to them.

Why did you start smoking again?

So, of these two classes of smoker, which has the greatest chance of success? The question is a no-brainer. It must be the person who realises that they did something wrong, wants to find out what it was and correct it. The other person has taken no responsibility for what is happening. The first person understands clearly that the decision to light up is in their power. And that is an important point. Whoever you are, if you have ever stopped smoking and started again remember...

It is you that lights the cigarette... nobody obliges you to do it. If you have ever stopped smoking and started again remember, that before you lit the cigarette, you had first mentally justified your action.

When we want to we can be both creative and convincing in our rationalizations, justifications and excuses. We have heard some marvellous ones: "How am I going put up with my husband if I cannot smoke?" or "I had to start smoking again; it was that or strangle the children." Taken at face value, they sound pretty convincing. Who in their right mind would advise strangling the children instead of smoking? No one! But was the choice a real one? I very much doubt it. It was just a way of justifying the desire to smoke. But that doesn't change the fact that it is just that, a justification, an excuse. So now, as we begin, it is very important that you take responsibility. To do this you first need to understand and accept that if you are reading this book, it is for entirely self-interested reasons (not selfish but self-interested). Smoking is selfish. Stopping smoking is self-interested. You want to be free of your addiction to nicotine. In other words you want to be a non-smoker. OK, it's a fact that those around you will be delighted and will enjoy the benefits of greater time spent in a smoke-free environment, but it is you who will accrue the greatest benefits. The benefits enjoyed by those around you will be no more than a reflection of the wonderful benefits that you enjoy.

Instruction number eight − Start with the right question: Usually when I tried to stop smoking I would give up within a few minutes or hours. Each time I tried to stop I would quickly start to feel panicky and questions would repeat themselves time and again in my mind, making me feel ever more anxious. The questions were always similar: "But how am I going to enjoy myself? Enjoy my coffee or a drink with friends?" My imagination would run wild: "How am going to face stressful situations? How am I going to have a poo in the morning? How am I going to be able to concentrate?" Perhaps you have experienced the same feelings, the same sense of dread. In reality, stopping smoking is marvellous. However, we feel like this because we have spent so many years smoking and we have forgotten what it feels like to be a non-smoker.

The above questions are not the best questions to ask yourself if you want to stop smoking. They are rooted in the fear which arises from the manipulated mental map of smoking, designed by the tobacco, and pharmaceutical industry that hooked us in the first place and keeps us hooked.

To solve any problem in life you must first ask the right question.

The right question is the following: "What makes me believe that I need to smoke? After all, humans are born as non-smokers. It is our natural state. Before we started smoking, we didn't feel that we needed or missed them. So what happened to me? What makes me now believe that I have to spend my life systematically poisoning myself, paying a fortune to do it, not just with money but with my health, wellbeing and freedom. The fact is that you don't have to do this any more.

It is quite likely that whilst you are reading this book, you will suddenly think, probably with a touch of anxiety, "But how am I going to drink my coffee tomorrow morning without a cigarette? Drive without a cigarette?… etc, etc." Whenever you catch yourself doing that, pause and change the question to…

"What makes me believe that I need to smoke whilst I'm drinking my coffee, etc…?

2

So why do smokers who get free start again?

So why, having stopped smoking, do smokers start again? It would be unbelievable if it didn't happen all the time. A smoker, after years of suffering the life of a nicotine addict, finally gets free. He frees himself of the drudgery of permanent bad breath, lack of vitality, the constant lying, feeling stupid, wheezing, snoring, premature aging, the constant fear and the thrall of addiction. He quickly begins to appreciate his better health, having more money in his pocket and most of all a sense of joy, of freedom. And then, some weeks, months or even years later he tries one ('just the one') and very soon finds himself back in the trap from which he was so happy to escape.

It is heart-breaking that so many people who were free, start again. The work of helping clients stop smoking sometimes feels like the task of Sisyphus. (In Greek mythology Sisyphus was a king, punished by being compelled to roll an immense boulder up a hill, only to watch it roll back down again and to repeat this throughout eternity.) There are only two reasons that a smoker falls back into the scam:

1. She believes that the cigarette does provide her with some sort of pleasure or benefit.
2. She believes that it is possible to control her consumption, that is to say smoke just those three or five 'special ones'.

So often a client who has got hooked again will say things like, "I was free, so happy, I didn't miss them, felt fantastic, I had started sports again; everything was going so well and then… I was at a wedding and thought that after so many years without smoking anything that I could risk just one cigar," or "I suffered a bad moment and I felt that I needed a cigarette," or "I was at a party and smoked a joint. I didn't think that it would count," "I thought that it was so easy to stop and that after so many years without smoking that I could control it. What I did was so stupid, I was wrong and here I am smoking the same or even more than I did when I stopped."

Usually, what the smoker was looking for when she lit that cigarette was something that doesn't and has never existed: *just one cigarette* and what she got was all that there ever truly was or will be: *the life of a smoker*, that is to say the very life that she was so sick of when she stopped smoking. It's that very same false idea, vain hope of smoking just one that got us hooked in the first place. There is simply no such thing.

So how is it that after freeing herself of the nightmare of a smoker's life, the constant bad breath, the fear, the lack of energy, the wasted money, the coughing, wheezing, headaches, the utter slavery and absurdness of it all, does she go right back and get hooked again?

The answer is straightforward: she doubted her decision.

Before we go any further, it is absolutely vital that you understand that there is no mystery. Before lighting that cigarette, our soon-to-be-enslaved-again smoker has rationalised and justified smoking that cigarette. You doubt that? Well ask yourself, "Who lit that cigarette?" You did. No one forced you to.

The fact is anyone can stop smoking and be delighted with life as a non-smoker. All you need to do is accept certain truths:

- That you don't enjoy being a smoker, you never did and you never will.
- There is not a single genuine benefit to be had from nicotine or tobacco. There is absolutely nothing to give up.
- There is no such thing as just one cigarette, an occasional or special cigarette — just the depression, disease and slavery of the life of a smoker.

Seems simple enough doesn't it? So why do so many smokers fail? To find the answer to that question we need to look at why we started in the first place.

3

So how did we get started in the first place?

Firstly; what is smoking? Smoking is an addiction to the nerve-toxin, nicotine. Addiction to any drug means to carry on taking that drug in spite of the negative, social, health and economic consequences and often against the rational judgement of the addict. All addictive drugs work in the same way. Nicotine is no exception. All addictive drugs create a feeling of emptiness in the addict who then mistakenly takes more of the drug to try and fill the emptiness that the drug itself created. The drug creates the need for itself. This can be seen very clearly with a drug like heroin. It is very clear that the addict takes his next dose not to feel marvellous but to put an end to the terrible withdrawal pangs suffered when the body eliminates the drug of the previous dose.

So why did we start in the first place? The answer is simple. We thought that we would get some benefit out of it: that it would make us more attractive, manlier, look rebellious, cool, that we would fit in better socially, that it would make us look older. Those are pretty big claims for any substance. It would seem ludicrous if for example, we tried to ascribe such benefits to eating bananas or mangoes. So where exactly did these ideas come from?

1. Indirect publicity — The media (primarily cinema).
2. Direct publicity — Advertising and sponsorship.
3. Environment — The people and information around you.

The tobacco industry has a problem. When its customers use its products exactly as they are supposed to, they will cause the premature death of about half of them. The other half will suffer an increasingly poor level of health and wellbeing. So, putting aside the moral aspect (*after all, the tobacco industry and their helpers, the PR industry* do) and given that it is the single largest cause of preventable disease in our society, the question must be how come we got started in the first place.

Firstly, if like me, you started smoking prior to the 1980's, no one told you beforehand that nicotine was a highly addictive drug, responsible for many horrific diseases and immense suffering. Instead, you probably felt it was cool, adult, just a habit, more or less normal and something that 'everyone did'. In fact, in order to try those first cigarettes, we had to be convinced that there were immense benefits to be had and very little, if any, danger. In fact, what we believed when we lit that first cigarette and what we believe most of our lives about tobacco and smokers is the exact opposite to reality.

How did this happen? How did we come to believe something that was and is the opposite to reality? Earlier, I wrote of mental maps and how they condition every aspect of our lives. They condition all aspects of our beliefs and perceptions. What this means is that by manipulating the mental map of a person in a certain way, you can get them to do absolutely anything you want, even if it is against their own interest – a powerful weapon indeed.

Extreme examples of this are suicide bombers. To get someone to kill themselves and others (usually innocent bystanders) takes a fair amount of manipulation. The astounding thing is that the families of the suicide bombers are often proud of the sacrifice of their son or daughter. Smokers are effectively the tobacco industry's suicide bombers. The PR industry acts as its recruiters and trainers. I recently watched an interview with some Jehovah's Witnesses, a couple whose child suffered and died because they would not allow it to receive treatment (a blood transfusion, because they believed it a sin. As a father I find this mind boggling. Just today I watched a video clip in which a fundamentalist American Christian was lecturing his audience about the demonic nature of yoga!! Then there is the manipulated mind map that makes perfectly rational people insist upon the genital mutilation of female and male children. How about the genocide in Rwanda? The list of barbarities committed by humans on other humans is horrific. What is always behind these are manipulated mental maps. The most common and practiced manipulators are 'big' industry, governments and religion.

During the study of the behaviour of a certain species of ant, some scientists noticed something strange in their behaviour. Ants were observed repeatedly climbing to the very tops of stalks of grass. Upon reaching the top they would fall off. Once on the ground, they would repeat the process, endlessly repeating the cycle. So what is in it for the ant? The answer is nothing at all. What is going on? Why does the ant keep doing it? The reason is that the ant has been infected by a parasite which spends the first part of its life-cycle in ants and the next part in herbivorous grazing animals (for example cows). Once the parasite has completed the first cycle of its existence (within the ant), it must find a way to enter the digestive system of the cow. This only occurs if it is eaten by the cow. If the ant can be manipulated into a position at the very

36

top of a blade of grass, it greatly increases the chance of this happening. The ant doesn't know why it feels compelled to repeatedly climb that blade of grass; it just feels that it is 'the right thing to do'. What the PR industry does, very effectively, is create and introduce dangerous infectious parasitic ideas into our minds, thereby turning us into hosts for big evil parasitic entities such as the tobacco industry.

This is achieved by the cynical manipulation of the mental maps and models that we all use to understand the world.

Practically all of what we believe – the good, the bad, in fact all that we take as real – has been introduced into our minds by our parents, teachers, friends (often with good intentions) and by government, television, the press, big industry, PR and advertising. (usually for profit or advantage). Many ideas and the things that we believe in, *things that we accept as facts, things that 'everyone knows' to be true* are not based on first-hand experience but belief. We accept many things without question. For example, we all know that the shape of our planet, the earth, is a sphere (oblate spheroid or geoid to give it a more accurate description). Have you ever proved that it is really so? Do you have incontrovertible first-hand experience of these facts? Almost certainly not. It's one of those 'everyone-knows-that' facts. But if you had asked the same question just five hundred years ago, the answer would have been delivered with equal certainty: "The earth is flat... everyone knows that." "Ah!" you say, "it's different nowadays. We live in a modern scientific age." Europeans have believed that they live in a modern scientific age for the past five hundred years (at least since the Renaissance). If we start to truly examine many of our beliefs, we find many of them are just things that we take for granted as an 'everybody-knows-that' fact.

Much of what 'everyone knows' to be true nowadays, will be superseded by better and more accurate models in the future. From the times of the ancient Greeks until only a hundred years ago it was accepted that the atom was the smallest particle of matter possible. Nowadays, we accept that there are many subatomic particles smaller than the atom. As modern and as scientific as we might believe ourselves to be, we are largely driven by primitive needs and desires. In the not too distant future many of our beliefs (our mental maps and models) about our world will be superseded by different and probably 'better' beliefs (mental maps and models).

There is absolutely nothing wrong with having mental maps. The danger exists in not knowing that they are just that: mental maps. Most of us call our own mental maps 'reality'. We usually don't question 'reality' because it's err... reality. Humans will fight to the death to defend something that is no more than a notion. Half the time we don't know where our beliefs come from. We probably haven't ever stopped to really examine them. Religious beliefs are a great example. I am not getting into whether or not God exists; simply that if you are born into a Muslim family, living in a Muslim society, then your beliefs, your mental models, are most probably Muslim. You 'know in your bones' that Islam is the true way. Not surprisingly, if you happen to be born into a Christian family in a Christian society then your idea of God will probably be Christian. You will know in your bones that Christ is the true way. On another scale we carry with us beliefs and mental maps about national stereotypes. There is the old joke which depends on this:

In heaven the police are British, the cooks are French, the engineers are German, the administrators are Swiss and the lovers are Italian. In hell the police are German, the cooks are British, the engineers are Italian, the administrators are French and the lovers are Swiss.

The joke works only because of our received opinions that go to create mental maps, not based on experience, but on what 'everyone knows'. However, history has shown that simply because everyone believes something, does not mean that it is true. In fact, I would argue that it usually means the opposite.

Another powerful aspect of our mental maps is that we tend to use them as a filter for the physical world. That is, we tend to reject whatever evidence does not support *our reality* and we exaggerate the importance of evidence that does support it. A good example of this is what I call the 'Uncle Nigel syndrome'. Most smokers have in their mind an 'Uncle Nigel' figure. Uncle Nigel lived well into his eighties, smoked two packs a day all of his life and was never ill. Most smokers will also know or have heard of someone, a friend of a neighbour, for example, who died of lung cancer without ever having smoked a cigarette in her life. We ignore the fact that Uncle Nigel was unusually lucky and that he would probably be alive today if he hadn't smoked. We also ignore the fact that more than 90% of lung cancer sufferers are or have been smokers. An important aspect of our mental models is that we work the facts so that they support the model. In other words, mental models are self-reinforcing.

I was born in 1957 into the 'Cold War' society, in which the USSR was perceived by most westerners as a constant threat — an evil empire. In 1989 I travelled to Moscow to take part in a seminar. It was just before the USSR imploded. Whilst there, I met and worked with citizens of the Soviet Union. I found the majority of the people I met to be very agreeable, kind, intelligent and exceptionally well-educated. During one conversation with a Russian university professor I said, "We, as people, get on well. I believe that our countries would get on much better if the Soviet Union were not so aggressive toward the West." She became quite agitated, saying, "It is not the Soviet Union that is aggressive toward the West; it is the West that is aggressive toward us, the Soviet Union." It quickly became clear that we each had a mental model firmly fixed in our heads that was the opposite to that held by the other. We had each been infected with a parasitic idea, crafted by our respective governments and the media to make us more pliable and manageable.

Those who have the resources and knowledge to shape our mental maps have immense power.

Many techniques employed in the massive mental manipulation that is found at all levels in our society were originally developed by Mr Edward Bernays (1891 – 1995), nephew of the famous psychologist Sigmund Freud. Edward Bernays is widely recognised as the founder of the modern PR/communications industry. He used the psychological ideas of his uncle as a basis to develop a variety of techniques (such as subliminal images) to manipulate our emotions and perceptions in order to change our mental maps – the beginnings of brainwashing. He managed to do this on a massive scale. We are subjected every single day to manipulation and brainwashing based upon the ideas and techniques invented by Bernays. They are now used by all industries and even governments to manipulate us (the 'War on Terror' being a prime example). The way in which these techniques have been abused by the PR industry on behalf of the tobacco, alcohol, pharmaceutical and food industry has had a particularly devastating impact on the health and wellbeing of us all. This is made even more effective by an education system that does not teach critical thinking.

Let's get back to the tobacco industry. I have asked thousands of people in my sessions, "Why did you start smoking?" Their reasons are similar to mine and yours and it nearly always related to image and social pressure: to look more mature or more attractive; out of curiosity; to fit in with a particular group of friends; to look tough and rebellious; to manage stress at university. Not once has someone said that he started smoking for the awful taste or smell of tobacco or because he wanted to cough or vomit. So where did these ideas come from? *The reality* of smoking is that it makes you smell like a giant ashtray; it's anti social; causes premature ageing, wheezing, lethargy, bad breath, horrific debilitating diseases, costs a fortune, dominates all aspects of your life and there is a fifty percent chance that it will kill you. How did we get from that, *the reality,* to believing that smoking makes us more attractive, that it's a sexual or social prop, that it gives us courage, that somehow it is cool to smoke, that it is edgy, that it helps us face stress and the difficult moments of life? If cigarettes really did all of those things then doctors would have an extremely easy life. Nicotine would be available on prescription. It would be so easy to recognise a smoker, as all smokers would be centred, relaxed, courageous, attractive and so totally cool. The tobacco industry which benefits financially from the death and suffering of its customers also has managed to corrupt politicians into watering down tobacco control laws, whilst simultaneously funding associations for the 'tolerance of smoking' to the point where thousands of non-smokers have suffered sickness and death from passive smoking, all in the name of co-existence and reasonableness.

Think about it for a moment; the accepted (manipulated) perceptions of addiction to nicotine (smoking) are exactly the opposite to reality. The fact is that we have been manipulated into these perceptions. The techniques developed by Bernays' successors in the PR industry (named by the comedian Bill Hicks as 'Devil's Spawn') have been used very effectively to shape and distort our perception of tobacco. Our mental maps (those of smokers and non-smokers alike) have been manipulated to suit the tobacco industry.

The objective of the tobacco industry is to get you hooked and squeeze every penny they can out of you before you die. All they need to do is convince you to try just a few experimental cigarettes. They do this by introducing a deadly parasitic idea into your mind.

Since birth and throughout our lives we are subjected to a constant and powerful stream of images, ideas and statements that prepare us for those first experimental cigarettes. As a child of 10 years old, I remember watching a film about a Mexican rebel. He was the hero fighting the fat, corrupt and cruel politicians for the rights of the downtrodden peasant. He was handsome, courageous and all the girls loved him. He robbed the rich to give to the poor. Inevitably he was captured. About to be executed, he bravely refused the blindfold and staring death in the face, he didn't blink; instead he requested a last cigarette. With immense dignity he took three drags of the cigarette, then turned to the firing squad and said, "I'm ready." Then they executed him. I was impressed and thought, "Wow what a hero!" I immediately wanted to be as brave as him in the face of danger. I wanted to smoke like Clint Eastwood and Humphrey Bogart. They were such tough guys. I even practiced smoking like them in front of the mirror.

Why did you start smoking again?

I remember also the famous 'after sex' cigarettes — Sean Connery as 007 seducing all those heroines during the sixties and seventies. There were no explicit sex scenes. Instead, just as things got interesting, the film would cut to a scene of Bond and his latest 'bit of stuff' lying side by side in bed, the woman with an expression on her face like the cat that got the cream. It was clear that she had just experienced the best bonk in her life. 007 at this point would light two cigarettes and give one to the girl. I thought that was so cool. I just couldn't wait to do the same.

In other films you see heroes smoking cigars to celebrate. We even have the spectacle of Sigourney Weaver, a main character, a heroine, in the film 'Avatar' smoking. What really caught my attention is that her smoking is inconsistent with almost any other aspect of the film. How many children will start smoking, inspired or helped along by this image? As much as I admire James Cameron as a director, I believe his attitude towards smoking to be irresponsible, considering the influence his films have on children.

What we don't realise, especially when we are young, is that it is not the cigarette that glamourises the person. It's the opposite; it is the person that glamourises the cigarette. (If you want more information about collusion between cinema and the tobacco industry, see Reference 6.)

Until recently in the Western world the tobacco industry sponsored sport. Can you think of anything more absurd? — linking nicotine addiction to glamour, fitness, health and success? (As I said earlier — the opposite to the truth.) The tobacco industry has sponsored, amongst other things, tennis, golf and Formula 1 racing. They have paid and still pay pretty girls to go around offering free cigarettes in bars. You probably remember the Marlboro adverts with their rugged, outdoor, healthy, attractive, 'real men' cowboys (again the opposite to reality). That image might seem a bit dated but during the fifties and sixties the tobacco industry used images that would not be allowed nowadays or would simply be laughed at: doctors in white coats, with a stethoscope around their neck, selling tobacco with the slogan 'Camel the brand preferred by doctors', or 'Craven A, better for your throat'. Doctors, a collective which inspires great trust, betrayed that trust and flogged tobacco. It all stinks of 'The Golden Rule'. It seems so obvious and so naïve when we see those ads now. What makes you believe that this sort of underhand dealing has stopped? It hasn't; it's just more sophisticated and subtle nowadays. You'd have to be naïve or just plain stupid to think that it hasn't.

Public, NGO and finally government pressure helped ensure that smoking in films almost disappeared during the nineties. It is back with a vengeance, as are the images of celebrities smoking. Older clients are often puzzled, saying something like, "I started because I didn't know any better but the youngsters today are warned; they have all the information about smoking; they know what a terrible thing smoking is. So why do they start?" It is simply because the new message crafted by the PR industry and transmitted so powerfully to unsuspecting adolescents is: *Smoking is cool, smoking is rebellious, smoking is glamorous, and to hell with the consequences.* It is difficult to imagine a more compelling message for an adolescent.

Coming back to you and me, how could we have protected ourselves? We didn't even know that we were being manipulated. Our parents and the adults we depended upon were also manipulated. The bodies set up to protect us, failed us. But not only did they fail us; many sold us out and then very handily also managed to blame us for being smokers. Having participated in getting us hooked and then taxed us to death (in many cases literally) on the price of tobacco, they now blame smokers for having fallen for the nicotine scam. Smokers nowadays are treated almost as lepers. Governments are constantly thinking of ways to frighten or further ostracise the smoker. This stinks. It doesn't even help you to stop. It might make you more desperate to stop but it doesn't help you do it. The reaction of many smokers to these tactics is to smoke more.

Finally we have those important figures in our lives. Mine was the head of upper school, Mr Peter Scahill, a lovely man, humane but hard as nails, tough on us all and responsible for outward bound activity. He was a heavy smoker who eventually died of lung cancer. To me he was a hero. To smoke was to be like him – tough and fair. The cigarette didn't make him any more tough or admirable but he unwittingly made the cigarette more attractive.

If you go through your own experience with your eyes open, you will see many similar examples of how the tobacco and PR industry introduced the parasitic idea into your mind during your own childhood and adolescent. Why? It was to get you to smoke those few experimental cigarettes. You never decided to be a smoker for the rest of your life. You just tried those first experimental cigarettes and that was enough.

We have talked about one of the psychological aspects of smoking, about just how the tobacco and PR industry have manipulated your and my perception and that of society as a whole. Their objective was to get the drug nicotine into our bodies.

42

Why did you start smoking again?

Now, cast your mind back to your first cigarette. Focus on the taste and physical effects. If you have any memory of that first cigarette, it is probable that it tasted horrible, strange, unpleasant and made you cough, feel dizzy and maybe even vomit. Why? Simple. Nicotine is a highly toxic substance and many additives in the cigarette are toxic and poisonous. Every creature on this planet has an inbuilt survival system. Part of this system has evolved to stop us from ingesting poison. For example, on my farm I do not have to explain to my horses what they may or may not eat; they already know, thanks to their survival system. If it tastes good, it's food. If it tastes bad, it's not food so don't eat it. That is precisely why the first cigarette tastes so awful: it was your body warning you: "Danger! Poison! Stop!" But thanks to that deadly parasitic idea introduced into our brains, we don't see it as a warning but as a challenge: "If I can just get over this bit, I will be sexier, more mature, more interesting. I'll be cool. It'll be easier to score."

Many rituals have evolved around learning to smoke. The most common one is to inhale the smoke, speak, then exhale through your nose. I worked so hard to learn this. It was a disgusting and sickening process but I was determined to show my companions that I was grown-up, a man. I had no idea that I, like many, had been infected with the parasitic idea. I just felt that I wanted the prize that had been promised. It was a lie. The prize never even existed.

However, as far as the tobacco industry is concerned, phase one has been successful: you have introduced the drug, the nerve-toxin nicotine into your body and the process of becoming a nicotine addict, a smoker has begun.

Addiction – how it works

It really does not matter what the drug might be, the process is the same. The addictive drug is introduced into the body which recognises it as a poison. The body eliminates the drug but in doing so creates an empty feeling in the user, who then puts more drug in his body to try to fill the emptiness that the drug itself created. The drug creates a need for itself.

Before we go any further we need to talk about nicotine withdrawal: the chemical process that lies at the heart of smoking, that is to say, nicotine addiction. Both the tobacco and pharmaceutical industry have invested millions in misleading smokers as to the true nature of nicotine withdrawal, so that they can sell them more nicotine. Let's talk about this now...

Geoffrey Molloy

4

What is physical nicotine withdrawal really?

The tobacco industry wants you, the smoker, to keep smoking. Playing up the severity of the nicotine withdrawal symptoms is a good way of doing just that. They are of course aided and abetted by the pharmaceutical industry and many of the medical profession. Having frightened the smoker senseless about the terrible withdrawal symptoms, they are able (by lucky coincidence perhaps?) to provide *their* drugs as the solution. The first of these drugs is – would you believe it – nicotine in the form of patches, gum or nasal-spray. The latest of these is the electronic cigarette. They have even conned the more gullible elements of the medical profession into using this treatment, cleverly misnaming it 'Nicotine Replacement Therapy'. It is in fact '*Cigarette* Replacement Therapy'. You do not free yourself of nicotine addiction; you simply change your drug supplier. Your pusher changes from the tobacco industry to the pharmaceutical industry, until, like 99% of smokers who try to stop smoking with pharmaceuticals, you start smoking again. I have seen so many clients who have used nicotine gum to stop smoking. Many stop smoking cigarettes but become addicted to the gum.

The second type of stop-smoking drug on the market are pills which act on your brain in a similar way to antidepressant drugs. The side effects can be much worse than the withdrawal symptoms they are supposed to help overcome. These side effects can even kill you or leave you permanently damaged. (I refer you again to Reference 4.)

Many smokers unnecessarily fear that they must suffer a terrible trauma in order to free themselves from their addiction. The cause of this fear is the misperception about the nicotine withdrawal – a misperception constantly reinforced by the pushers – the tobacco industry and the pharmaceutical industry.

The very way it has been named for example, is enough to provoke fear: 'nicotine withdrawal pangs'. Any experience, the description of which includes the word 'pangs' is quite likely to cause err... pangs of anxiety. (Synonyms for the word 'pangs' include: agony, anguish, misery, and distress.) Even if you never thought about withdrawal pangs, now you know that you are going to experience something terrible known as

45

'nicotine withdrawal pangs', you're sure going to be on the look out for them. When you talk to your friends, what word will you use to describe your experience? Why, the expression 'withdrawal pangs' perhaps? For many smokers, just thinking about the pangs that they're going to have to go through, is enough to make them feel err... pangs. The physical sensation of the body metabolizing and eliminating nicotine has probably been misnamed on purpose. These are the very same 'pangs' smokers live with 24 hours a day. They are what keep them smoking. And yet they are so weak that we have all have managed to get a good night's sleep in spite of them. Let's put it another way: these withdrawal pangs are so light that they don't even wake you up whilst you're asleep. However, it is the fear and misunderstanding of these mysterious 'withdrawal pangs' that keeps many smokers too frightened to try to stop.

In Spain the favourite expression is 'síndrome de abstinencia' (abstinence syndrome) and is another great way to keep us wrong-footed. Checking the dictionary I find that the synonyms for the verb 'to abstain' include: deprive oneself of, give up, do with out, refrain from. So if you didn't think that there was something to sacrifice, then the use of the expression 'to abstain' will help change that. 'To abstain' implies directly that you are making some sort of sacrifice even if it might be a sacrifice to achieve some greater good. Perhaps the best known example of the effectiveness of abstinence is sex. Pope Benedict XIII and many before him have made it clear that we should abstain from sex outside marriage. Even in Spain and Ireland, two strongly Catholic countries, the idea of abstaining has been spectacularly unsuccessful. (Not even the altar boys are safe from priests unable to abstain!) Even in countries such as Afghanistan and Iran, where the penalty for non-abstinence (illicit sex) is frequently a horrific, painful public execution by stoning, people are still unable to abstain. Why? The idea of abstinence is synonymous with sacrifice and giving up. It implies that you have to sacrifice a genuine pleasure or help in life perhaps for some greater good – Lent, for example. The effect is to make something instantly more attractive. This is clearly an expression that does not apply to stopping smoking. Smoking in fact provides the smoker with not one single benefit. The idea of abstaining does not apply to stopping smoking as there is nothing to sacrifice or give up.

In this book when I talk about the physical withdrawal symptoms, I am not referring to the great drama, suffering and bad temper that smokers suffer when they try to stop smoking 'por cojones'. Throughout this book I use this expression. There are expressions in each language which communicate a sense or an idea which cannot be translated accurately and concisely into another language. 'Por cojones' implies a white-knuckled, will-power of steel approach but thrown in, there is a certain sense of 'bravura' of a slightly 'macho' flavour.

The physical withdrawal is just that: *physical*. It is not a 'habit' nor is it 'psychological', it's just a sensation one feels more or less in the area of the solar plexus/stomach. It is a side-effect of the body metabolising and eliminating nicotine. (For more information about nicotine and its effect on the human organism, see Reference 5.)

Once you have put out your last cigarette, it takes the body from three to five days to eliminate nicotine. Thus, the physical withdrawal lasts between three and five days. (We'll say up to five days, just to allow for any possible margin of error.) Once nicotine has been eliminated from the body, it is no longer possible to experience physical withdrawal symptoms.

The physical withdrawal symptoms are what smokers have lived with since they started smoking as children or young adults – at school, university or during military service, for example. Most smokers will not have experienced adult life without this constant physical withdrawal feeling for nicotine. It is like a background noise to which you've become so accustomed that most of the time it is invisible to you, or if you are aware of it, you usually mistake it for something else like nerves, stress or hunger. It is a sense of there being something missing, a light discomfort, a niggling sort of irritation.

Even given all of those clues, you still may not be able to identify it – it is that light. It is similar to the feeling of normal hunger. There are times when I don't get to eat for most of the day. I survive without any pain but I have observed that after too long a time without food (especially if there is food available but I cannot eat for whatever reason), I find myself becoming more irritable, less able to concentrate. This is very similar to what happens with the physical withdrawal symptoms for nicotine. A typical comment made by our clients after stopping smoking with us is that the physical withdrawal symptoms were surprisingly light or non-existent. These exclamations of surprise are usually made by the smokers who had suffered the most in their previous attempts. However, once they get their ideas clear, they simply cannot believe just how easy it is.

So, if you're worried about the infamous withdrawal pangs, relax. What you will find (if you don't already know it), is that the physical withdrawal is, in fact, very light. Smokers have been smoking and dying for generations without knowing that they have been addicted to a drug. When I started smoking at the end of the sixties, smoking was called a habit. Drugs such as heroin were regarded as 'addictive drugs' but smoking was a 'habit'. The first suspicions that nicotine was an addictive drug were being voiced at the same time as the tobacco companies were claiming that nicotine was not addictive. They got away with this for a long time by muddying the waters, mostly through cleverly crafted lies and half truths (a tactic first perfected by the tobacco industry and now used by many other big industries.) They claimed that nicotine could not be addictive because there is no detectable stupefying effect that you might get, for example, with alcohol or heroin. (*Interestingly, at the same time as they made these declarations they were also perfecting the use of ammonia to increase the effect of nicotine and its delivery in the human body. This results in increasing the tolerance of the body to nicotine which in turn leads to the smoker smoking more – filling the coffers of the tobacco industry ever more.*) In the sixties and seventies most young men smoked. Everyone 'knew' that smoking was a habit.

The withdrawal is so light that many smokers only recognise the withdrawal as a thought: "I want or I feel like a cigarette." The suffering and dramas that smokers go through when they try stopping smoking 'por cojones' is 98% psychological. However, one of the favourite topics of conversation with at least half of the smokers in any session we give are descriptions of the terrible withdrawal pangs they suffered in previous attempts to stop smoking. They confuse the purely physical with what's going on in their mind.

5

If the withdrawal is so light, why does everyone talk about how strong it is?

It is because we confuse the cause with the symptoms. As I wrote earlier, the physical sensation is so light that it doesn't even wake you up when you're asleep. Many smokers can go hours without smoking. Many smokers have clearly defined situations in which they simply don't smoke. Many won't smoke in front of their children; others never in front of their parents and others never in front of non-smokers or never on aeroplane flights. Think for a moment. If the withdrawal were so strong, it would simply be impossible to not smoke in these situations. Think! When the mind isn't involved, when you are asleep for example, the withdrawal is of no consequence at all because at a physical level it is so very light. It is only when the mind gets involved that things start to go really wrong.

How do addictive drugs work?

Nicotine is an addictive drug in the same way that heroin is an addictive drug. Every addictive drug has its unique characteristics. There are two principal phases: the psychotropic effect of the drug (the effect the drug has upon you whilst you are 'under the influence' – in the case of nicotine, whilst you are smoking) and secondly, the withdrawal phase when the body eliminates the drug (the time between cigarettes).

The process by which the drug user becomes addicted and thus a slave to the drug is identical for all drugs. In essence, every addictive drug creates a hole, a sensation of emptiness in the addict and the addict mistakenly feels the need to put more drug in her body to try and fill the emptiness that the drug itself created.

To understand how this process works, it's important that we understand some basic mechanisms in the human body.

The strongest desire that any creature on this planet has is the drive to survive and to be at the best level of wellbeing possible. Every aspect of our behaviour, everything we do is either directly or indirectly to achieve that end. Responsible for regulating all of this activity is an area of the brain known as the hypothalamus. For our purposes, we can divide its activities into two areas:

Internal environment: Survival in its most basic form means maintaining a balanced internal environment in our bodies to ensure correct functioning. Our bodies can only work efficiently within certain limits and these must be controlled to respond to our constantly changing external environment. For example, the chemical processes in our bodies work best at a certain temperature 37.0°C, and at pH of 7.36 (level of alkalinity/acidity). Other aspects that also need to be controlled are blood-sugar levels and hydration. Our marvellous survival mechanism ensures that if we are nearing the edge of these limits, we begin to feel uncomfortable until we take corrective action. For example, if we feel too cold we feel uncomfortable until we put on more clothing. If we have low blood-sugar we feel hungry until we eat. If we are dehydrated we feel thirsty until we drink.

External threats: Survival also means keeping ourselves safe from possible danger and threats to our wellbeing. In its most primitive form, it meant keeping ourselves safe from animals that wanted to eat us. To visualise this working, imagine that you are out walking in the country and suddenly find yourself face to face with a hungry bear. You suspect that the bear is thinking something like, "Hmmmm, now he looks like something good to eat!" It is vital that you are able to react quickly and effectively. Your survival, your very life, depends upon it.

You receive all information about events in the physical world through your senses. However, this is raw data and means nothing until it is ordered and interpreted in your mind, using your mental models. If something occurs which is perceived within your mental model as dangerous or life-threatening, your brain sends a signal to the hypothalamus which, in turn, produces powerful chemical changes in your body (secreting adrenaline and cortisol, for example). You will suddenly find yourself experiencing fear which is so uncomfortable that you will feel moved to either fight or run away. Included in these physical changes are increased heart rate, more rapid breathing, higher blood pressure; the pupils dilate and digestion stops. An important aspect of the hypothalamus is that it reacts not only to events but to thoughts as well. Just imagining a dangerous situation can produce the same physical response as a real dangerous situation. In the modern world perhaps the most common place that we experience this reaction is on the road – a fright whilst you're driving, for example.

Why did you start smoking again?

This survival system is magnificent. Take hunger, for example. Hunger is not a habit or psychological, it is chemical. When you need food, chemical changes in your blood-stream inform your brain that you need to eat. The feeling of normal hunger is not painful; it is an empty, slightly insecure feeling. We can feel hungry and still get on with our lives. Eventually, the discomfort reaches a level that eating becomes a priority, especially if good food is to hand. In fact, the feeling of hunger is often so light that it is only when the smell of food reaches your nose (meaning that ending the hunger becomes possible) that you suddenly become aware of your hunger and again eating becomes a priority. The mechanism is marvellous, ensuring that you eat (keep your body fuelled up), without causing you pain. In fact, almost all survival signals are like this – although not painful, they are nevertheless powerfully coercive.

There are two important nerve centres in our bodies. The one that we all know about is our brain; it is also the seat of consciousness. The second lies in our gut. This is where a lot of the survival stuff, the regulating mechanisms, are centred but there is no consciousness there. However, we tend to 'feel' a lot of our survival signals there. For example, fear, anxiety, hunger, stress, all create an empty insecure feeling in the gut. A similar feeling is created when nicotine is metabolised and eliminated from the body.

We start smoking because of the mental manipulation, because of the evil parasitic idea that was introduced into our brains without us even realizing it. What makes smoking even more attractive to an adolescent is that it is a prohibited adult pleasure. During adolescence we yearn to be older, sexier, more confident. The manipulation that we have been subjected to since birth means that when we reach the insecure adolescent phase of our lives and are looking about for an image, a prop – the cigarette has already been established as a suitable candidate.

We try our first cigarette. None of us decided in that moment to become a smoker for the rest of our lives. The decision was just to smoke an experimental cigarette. Our survival system helps us to avoid getting poisoned. If something tastes horrible or smells horrible, produces a horrible reaction when ingested, this is your body's way of telling you that you are being poisoned. The first cigarettes taste horrible; they make us cough and feel dizzy; might even make us vomit. Your body is sending a clear message: "Aaaarghhh! you're poisoning me! Stop it now!"

If we hadn't already been infected by the parasitic idea, then that would be the end of the story. However, what happens is that all of the millions invested by the tobacco industry, all of the evil work of the PR industry to develop and implant the parasitic idea into our minds now

51

kicks in, helped of course by apathetic, spineless or collusive governments. In spite of this awful first experience we, as insecure adolescents, yearn for the marvellous benefits promised — in reality, all evil, cynical lies. We want to be more confident, sexier, grown-up, fun and attractive. In this light, the horrible first effects of smoking are seen as some kind of challenge, something we have to overcome if we want to feel more attractive, adult, sexy and fun. When I started, the acid-test within my group of friends was to be able to inhale the smoke, speak (we had to say "Archbishop Makarios"), then exhale the smoke through our nostrils. How diligently I applied myself and how I suffered in order to learn to do that! What nausea! How I coughed! I felt as sick as a parrot. The mental manipulation is so effective that when, after much suffering and nausea, I finally managed to tolerate the foul smell, the horrible taste, and the horrible effect on my body, I felt pleased with myself for being 'adult'.

If you haven't lived as a hermit in a cave, then you will have probably already heard that smoking is very bad and that it can kill you. You might even know of a family member or neighbour with a permanent cough or another who is suffering obvious symptoms of a smoking related disease. However, that first cigarette smells and tastes so revolting that we simply can't imagine that we will get hooked. We either think nothing at all or something like, "This tastes like shit! There is absolutely no way that I'll get hooked on this crap!" The horrible experience serves to create a completely false sense of security. What is certain is that nobody, when they smoke that first cigarette, thinks, "This cigarette is the first of the 500,000 cigarettes that I intend to smoke," or "From now on I'm going to smoke all day, every day, until they make me smell bad, make me live in constant fear, ruin my health and finally kill me!" We think that we are just smoking some experimental cigarettes and "anyway as we are still young, we still have plenty of time to stop." Even if what they say about smoking being dangerous is true, we feel that we can do it just a bit and will have stopped long before any of those horrible diseases can affect us.

When you put out that first cigarette, your body eliminates the drug and you experience a slightly empty, insecure feeling — something that you don't immediately notice; after all, insecurity is a more or less constant companion during the adolescent phase of our lives. If you light a cigarette during nicotine withdrawal, what you notice now is that when you light the cigarette, you do somehow feel better, slightly more relaxed, a bit more confident. This is not an illusion; you really do feel better than you did just a moment ago but the reason that you feel better is that the first cigarette made you feel worse (as the nicotine is eliminated from your body). You just couldn't see it. But of course, sooner or later you have to put out the cigarette and now you create the next empty, insecure feeling. Again you don't notice this feeling slowly growing inside you as it is masked by normal feelings of insecurity. But what you do notice is that you do feel better when you light the next cigarette. The manipulation of your mental model, that is the parasitic ideas planted in your mind, is now reinforced by the nicotine parasite that you have introduced into your body with the first cigarette and very soon, you are hooked.

Gradually, smoking becomes not just a 'pleasure' but an obligation. You don't exactly know why smoking is so important for you but it does seem to help. It seems to help in difficult times and to act as a prize in good times. You soon reach a point that it becomes vital to have cigarettes to hand at all times. You cannot imagine being in a social situation without smoking; you simply don't feel comfortable without them. You are now systematically poisoning your body. Your body tries to defend itself by creating more tolerance to the drug nicotine.

Acquired tolerance is another survival defence mechanism. If we are constantly exposed to a toxin, our bodies are capable of adapting to protect us. You have probably experienced acquired tolerance with alcohol and/or coffee. At 16 years old a single beer might leave you all squiffy but a few years on you need considerably more than a single beer to achieve the same squiffy effect. The same now occurs with nicotine. Your body adapts to protect you. This means that the same size dose of nicotine has less effect. In other words, now when you smoke a cigarette, you cannot completely relieve the insecurity caused by the previous cigarette and it leaves you feeling unsatisfied. This is where smokers are at a real disadvantage compared with heroin addicts.

Heroin addicts can see from early on that when they are between fixes they suffer heroin withdrawal. Heroin withdrawal is strong, rather like having a bad bout of flu. The same good friend who inspired me to finally stop smoking told me that she had also experimented with heroin (years ago when she was still very young), but stopped when she realised that the heroin withdrawal was becoming ever stronger. She also realised that, no matter how much heroin she took, she always needed greater doses and with greater frequency.

The smoker, on the other hand, is hardly aware of nicotine withdrawal. He lives with it 24 hours a day for the whole of his smoking life. His experience of nicotine withdrawal is simply a thought: "I want a cigarette." Unlike the heroin addict who can see that the withdrawal is getting stronger and requires ever larger doses of heroin to relieve it, if the smoker is aware of anything, it is simply that he wants a cigarette ever more frequently. But by smoking more, his body becomes even more tolerant to nicotine and the relief he experiences is ever smaller and the need to smoke seems ever greater. For the engineers among you reading this, you have created a 'positive feedback loop'. You try to correct the situation by putting more nicotine into the system but instead, after the initial relief, you actually feel worse and so smoke more, moving ever further away from the equilibrium that you seek. We see a similar process in our horses on our farm.

Our horses have to be purged of parasites regularly. You can think of the parasites like a tape-worm that get into the digestive system of the horses as tiny eggs on the grass they eat. A horse that is infected with such parasites cannot help but eat compulsively. The horse doesn't realise that he has a parasite inside him; he just knows that he feels hungry. The parasite needs nutrition to grow and hijacks the horse's survival mechanism to feed itself. However, as much as the horse eats, it is not enough. He eats to put an end to his hunger but each time he eats he is in fact making the parasite bigger and thus hungrier, which obliges the horse to eat even more. The horse gradually becomes less energetic and thinner and more susceptible to disease (whilst the parasite gets bigger and stronger and hungrier). The horse has less energy and is less able to resist the parasite. Horses can eventually die if not treated. And what does the parasite give the horse in return for all of this suffering? Exactly the same as the smoker gets for all of his suffering: ***Nothing. Not a single thing.***

Each smoker is doomed to suffer this disgusting, debilitating and deadly process. There is nothing else. It is all that addiction to nicotine (smoking) really is. The smoker will continue to smoke in the attempt to relieve the nicotine withdrawal caused by the previous cigarette but, although he feels a momentary relief of the withdrawal, the overall effect is to make it worse: smoking more, becoming more tolerant, getting ever less relief, whilst feeling an ever increasing need to smoke. Soon, the amount of nicotine that the smoker needs to relieve the discomfort of withdrawal exceeds the physical resistance of his body. The smoker has now reached the logical limit of this process which is simply the physical capacity of his body to cope with the systematic poisoning. All smokers reach this point: smoking the most that their bodies can stand, whilst being unable to completely eliminate the discomfort of nicotine withdrawal. For some smokers this physical limit might be two packs a day; for others it's just five cigarettes a day. The point being that the smoker now smokes all that his body can stand but in spite of this, he continues to suffer the constant, empty feeling of nicotine withdrawal.

Why did you start smoking again?

This is when the smoker experiences confusing phenomena such as putting out a cigarette and then just a few minutes later, even knowing that he has just smoked, feels that he hasn't. Or he lights a cigarette and realises that he already has a lighted cigarette in the ashtray. What frequently happened to me was feeling that the cigarette I was smoking wasn't 'enough' and then smoking another straight away. Once you get to the stage of constant withdrawal, you cannot ever completely fill the emptiness. For the smoker it is no longer a question of wanting or not wanting a cigarette; it is a question of organising his life according to the next opportunity to smoke. All smokers that have reached this stage will have their everyday life planned around the various opportunities they have to smoke: with or after breakfast, another on the way to work, a quick one before going into work, another at a mid-morning break, a couple at lunch time and so on. If there is any doubt about the next opportunity to smoke we will smoke an extra one 'just in case', even if it tastes like shit.

As I wrote earlier, the smoker does not identify the empty, insecure feeling as nicotine withdrawal. The sensation created by nicotine withdrawal is similar to the sensation of insecurity or anxiety that we feel when we are stressed, worried or anxious. The smoker, conditioned by the parasitic ideas (the mental manipulation), mistakenly feels that a cigarette helps him to relax in stressful moments and is a little reward in social moments.

Sooner or later, he experiences a desire to stop smoking. Perhaps, he has smoked far too much on a Saturday night; or it is the realization that smoking is affecting his sporting performance; or a person close to him suffers some horrible smoking related disease. However, the moment he thinks about stopping smoking, he feels panic − a dark fear, what I call the black hole syndrome. Remember, we usually start smoking very young. This means that we have never lived as adults without the constant emptiness of nicotine withdrawal. We mistakenly believe that this empty feeling is caused by life; that it is the emptiness that comes with being alive. When the smoker thinks of stopping smoking he feels panic. He thinks something like, "How am I going to fill that terrible emptiness without the cigarette to help me?" This is the fundamental and deadly misconception of all nicotine addicts (smokers). What the smoker does not see is that:

It is not the cigarette that fills the emptiness; it is the cigarette which causes the emptiness. The empty feeling is nicotine withdrawal.

The panic and anxiety that the smoker feels when he thinks about stopping smoking is 2% physical withdrawal and 98% fear. Some smokers have said, "Well that sounds like a good explanation but the panic and the physical anxiety that I experience when I stop smoking is not imaginary; it is very real." So, if nicotine withdrawal is so light, why do so many people suffer such dramas when they stop smoking?

The fact is that you largely get what you expect. I have a great example. Some years ago an attractive and intelligent nurse came to a stop-smoking session. She was a heavy smoker, habitually smoking two packs a day. She recounted the following anecdote:

After working for many years on the day-shift in a hospital, a job in which it was permitted to nip out and smoke, she changed jobs to work a night-shift at a different hospital. An important aspect of her new job was that for eight hours at a time, there would be no possibility of nipping out for a smoke. She was worried, as during previous attempts to stop or refrain from smoking she had 'gone up the wall' and as a consequence, started smoking again. Wanting the job but worried about not smoking for eight hours straight, she bought some nicotine patches. Her reasoning was that the patches would keep her sufficiently dosed up with nicotine and thus reduce the severity of nicotine withdrawal to a bearable level. At the beginning of her shift, whilst she changed into her uniform, she stuck a 'heavy-duty' nicotine patch on her thigh. The eight-hour shift passed. She did not smoke and was not aware of any sort of physical withdrawal. She admitted that she felt a little 'different' but was not alarmed as she put it down to the different way nicotine was administered to her body (nicotine patch instead of cigarette). At the end of her shift she felt pleased with herself. She was pleased that her strategy had been so effective. She was convinced that, thanks to the nicotine patch, she had passed the eight hours without any sort of suffering. It was only when she came to change out of her work clothes that she realised that the nicotine patch had come off her thigh and was in fact stuck to the inside of her trousers. She calculated that this must have happened as she was putting on her uniform, which meant that she had worked the eight hours without nicotine and without suffering. In that moment she realised that the physical withdrawal was not the real problem and that much of the suffering she had experienced previously had been in her mind. Up to that point, although many of her friends had stopped smoking with us, she was sceptical, believing that without medical help with the physical withdrawal, stopping smoking would be difficult for her, if not impossible. Her experience served to show her that the physical withdrawal is 2% of the problem and that by far the biggest suffering was the fear of something that simply did not exist, except in her mind. She stopped smoking in the session and was delighted to be free.

Nicotine withdrawal is no more than a slightly empty insecure feeling. It is similar to the normal sensation of hunger. Normal hunger is just an empty, insecure feeling which causes no pain. It is nevertheless strong enough to make sure that you eat. It forms part of our survival mechanism.

When you stop smoking *por cojones*, that is to say using the wrong, mental map, you feel that you have been forced to give up a pleasure or support and as a result you are annoyed and irritated about the sacrifice. You behave rather like a spoilt child, feeling that it's 'not fair', after all, it's your one little pleasure, your companion or consolation and "I'm not even allowed that!" Also, you feel increasingly anxious about just how you will be able to face certain situations without your drug to help you. You expect it to be difficult and you just know that you will suffer 'terrible nicotine withdrawal pangs' which can only be relieved by the cigarette. Obviously, you don't want to suffer any sort of withdrawal pangs but the belief that that you will makes you feel even more anxious. But this discomfort, whilst physical, is not caused by the body eliminating nicotine. It is caused by the fear of what might happen, by the mistaken ideas we have about life without a cigarette. I am not saying that the anxiety suffered by a smoker trying to stop *por cojones* is imaginary. The symptoms are real but it is the cause of these symptoms that is imaginary. In other words, the anxiety is created by the way we think. Perhaps that sounds a bit odd to you. How can the symptoms be real if the cause is imaginary?

There is causal relationship between mind and body. That is to say the chemical state of your body affects the way you think and the way in which you perceive the world. For example, I love riding my horse Chico and often ride in the nature reserve near to my home in Cantabria (in the north of Spain). On one occasion I was riding along a narrow path with a fairly sheer drop of a couple of hundred metres on the left side. I wasn't worried as I have spent years riding Chico and we each are confident of the other. We came to a gully which was difficult to cross. During the manoeuvre, Chico (who weighs close on 500 kilos) nearly fell on top of me. That gave me quite a scare. For an instant I experienced my own mortality. After the incident we carried on along the same narrow path. The drop on the left-hand side now felt considerably more dangerous. I was now aware that I felt more afraid. Nothing had changed, except the

57

state of my body. I was still charged up with adrenaline. The chemical state of my body altered my perception.

It works the other way too: what you think affects the state of your body. The hypothalamus cannot distinguish between events in the physical world and thinking about events in the physical world. Your brain will try to prepare your body for the situation whether it be real or imagined. This can easily be demonstrated with something as simple as a sexual fantasy. A sexual fantasy can easily produce an erection in a man. His circumstances have not changed and yet a simple thought has produced an important change in his body. His body responds to his thoughts.

Another example is one I am sure that we have all experienced: the frustration of the worrying thought that enters your mind at 3 a.m. and prevents you from sleeping. You feel tired and know that you need to sleep but your body feels restless and fidgety. You can tell that the last thing that your body feels like doing is sleeping. The anxious thought produces a corresponding anxious state in the body. Knowing that you cannot sleep and that you will probably feel tired for that important meeting the next day can make you feel even more anxious and even less likely to fall asleep.

The nurse described above was an obviously intelligent person. When she tried to stop smoking previously she had suffered 'terrible nicotine withdrawal pangs' and that is why she believed that introducing nicotine into her body would help reduce them. What became clear is that the intensity of the withdrawal pangs that she experienced was largely unrelated to her body eliminating nicotine. Her belief that she was wearing a nicotine patch was enough to eliminate the fear and anxiety she normally felt when she couldn't smoke; that is the fear of facing life without her pleasure or consolation and the idea that nicotine withdrawal would be both unpleasant and intense.

Addiction to nicotine is no different from any other drug addiction. The problem is in the mind of the addict. "Ah!" you say, "What about heroin withdrawal?" Until I started working with heroin addicts (something I no longer do), I too believed that heroin withdrawal was special and so bad that it made heroin different. The heroin addicts with whom I've worked have described the withdrawal as similar to having a very bad bout of flu. Think for a moment, if you had a choice of suffering a week of very bad flu on the one hand or losing everything — family, job, self-respect — on the other, which would you choose? The question is a no-brainer. Even in the case of heroin addiction, the problem is in the way the addict perceives the drug: the manipulated beliefs that he has about what the drug does for him and the fear of what he imagines might happen if he cannot have the drug.

A big mistake in our society has been to classify addiction as a physical illness to be treated by doctors. This misconception of the problem has been enthusiastically supported by the pharmaceutical industry who of course sells the drugs to treat the symptoms misdiagnosed as the cause. National and private health services around the world have wasted literally hundreds of millions of euros/dollars etc. on addiction treatment that is not and cannot be effective. You cannot change a drug addict's beliefs or perceptions of a drug with a pill or by giving him more of the very drug that causes the addiction in the first place.

Geoffrey Molloy

6

Deeper into the nightmare

The smoker feels trapped. He didn't mean to become a smoker, just try a few cigarettes but subtly, without realising what was happening, he has become hooked, a smoker, a nicotine addict. Each time he tries to stop or even thinks of stopping smoking, he feels fear. He is also frightened of carrying on smoking because he realizes that it is controlling his life, ruining his health and could even kill him. He is now trapped between opposing fears. He is frightened of stopping smoking and frightened about what will happen if he carries on.

So what does the smoker do? He has to carry on with his life. In order to deal with the anxiety and fear and to keep functioning, he begins to rationalize. What does rationalization mean in this context? Basically, it is lying. As I mentioned before, white lies are the lies that we tell to others so that they feel better. Rationalization is the act of lying to ourselves so that *we* feel better. If we were not able to rationalize then we would very likely become paralysed with fear. The problem is that very quickly we start to believe our own lies. It's not difficult as our minds are constantly manipulated by cinema, television etc, which serves to reinforce the original parasitic idea. Nor are we helped by the complicity that exists between smokers, each supporting the other: "Smokers are OK. People who don't smoke simply don't know how to enjoy themselves." "Huh! they'll be making sex illegal next!" etc, etc…

The biggest fear we have is that we will never be able to stop. Many smokers, just as I did, promise themselves almost every night, "Right, that's it! Tomorrow I'm stopping smoking." Of course, that's easy to say at the end of the day when you are absolutely saturated with nicotine and all of the other toxic components of cigarette smoke and you feel sick and tired of feeling sick and tired. But the following morning you don't feel so physically sick and the sensation of nicotine withdrawal has increased. (If you have slept for eight hours, your nicotine level is down to about 3% of what it was when you went to sleep.) It now just seems too difficult. To avoid the self-loathing that the failed attempt generates, the smoker probably tries to rationalize it: "Well, that wasn't a serious attempt to stop. I'll make a *serious* attempt next week or at Easter or during my holidays." However, the damage is done. The smoker feels in his heart that he can't stop smoking, even though he knows it's stupid to smoke. To make things worse, it seems that everyone feels that they have the right or even the mission to persecute smokers nowadays. Your children plead for you to stop smoking; your partner nags you; your friends tell you that you should stop smoking. Your doctor never misses an opportunity to tell you to stop. Complete strangers pull a disgusted face and wave a hand in front of their faces when you light up. The smoker is bullied, nagged, humiliated, vilified, criticized and made to feel like some sort of leper. He follows the only course open to him: he adopts a defensive posture and starts saying things like, "I absolutely love smoking!" "Everything causes cancer nowadays," "What's the point in stopping with all this pollution around," "Life's not worth living without its little pleasures!"

In effect, he now makes a Faustian pact — in other words, a pact with the devil. He says to himself something like this: "I know that smoking is disgusting, dangerous and costs me a fortune but at least it helps me with this emptiness; at least it helps me face the stress and strain of life." His fear is based on that misconception. *Remember, the feeling of emptiness and insecurity is the nicotine withdrawal. The cigarette doesn't fill that emptiness; it is the cause of that emptiness.* One of the many marvellous aspects of stopping smoking is to be free of that constant, niggling, empty feeling. After a few years of smoking we come to believe our own lies. The fear drives us even to fiercely defend our smoking. This reminds me of the following Taoist story:

A man had the habit of taking his coffee in the morning on the porch of his house whilst watching the world go by. Each day, as he stood on his porch drinking his coffee, he saw a large dog walk by. The dog was very big, had beautiful shiny golden fur and walked with a plucky gait. He was reminded of a dog he had loved as a child. He looked forward to seeing the dog each morning and the dog soon became part of his day. One day he noticed that the dog didn't walk with as much energy as he had before; it seemed less happy. He continued to watch the dog walk past his house each morning. He was alarmed to note that the dog was becoming sicker and sicker. Not only did the dog look tired; his fur was no longer shiny. The dog's health continued to deteriorate. After some weeks it had started to lose patches of hair and instead of fur there were now angry looking sores. The man became increasingly concerned over the state of the dog and one day he decided to follow him. He followed the dog some way until the dog came to place where he dug up a bone and started chewing on it. The man was alarmed; he could see that as the dog chewed the bone, so blood would flow from his mouth. As he looked closer he could see that the bone the dog was chewing was covered in sharp points and that the blood came from lacerations to the dog's mouth and gums caused by the bone. In spite of this, the dog chewed with what was clearly great gusto. The man, horrified, tried to take the bone from the dog but the dog growled at him, protecting the bone. The man was confused as to why the dog would behave in such a way, protecting something that was clearly doing him so much harm. Then in a flash he realised what was happening. The dog mistakenly believed that the blood he savoured came from the bone and so did all he could to protect it. The dog was convinced that the bone was a source of pleasure and something that he needed. In fact, the dog was consuming himself. The blood he savoured was his own.

Fortunately there is a big difference between the dog in this story and the smoker. The dog is doomed, he doesn't know any better, he cannot know any better. The smoker, on the other hand, has the intelligence to be able to put himself 'outside' the problem, analyse it and understand what is happening. To see the whole scam for what it is. To see that it is all an illusion – that there is absolutely nothing to give up. In that moment he has the possibility of truly freeing himself.

You may be reading this thinking, "Yes, but! Yes, but it really is a pleasure in certain moments or it really does help me relax, concentrate," etc.

OK, let's look at some of these so-called special cigarettes so that we really understand what causes these illusions.

The after-the-meal cigarette: This is the number one favourite cigarette for many smokers. A few years ago I spent a week in the UK during Christmas. I attended a Christmas dinner for about 120 people. We were seated at four long tables. I hadn't visited the UK for many years and was curious to see what changes there had been in smoking and smokers since my last visit. By custom, smoking was permitted only once the meal had finished. As we came to the end of the meal I was curious to know just how many smokers would light up. I waited and watched. After five minutes no one was smoking. After a few more minutes still no one had lit up. I began to think, "Wow, things have really changed here, it seems that no one smokes in the UK anymore!" However, a couple of minutes later, a man at the end of my table lit up and this started a chain reaction. Within a matter of seconds another 35 or more smokers lit up. The great relief of being able to smoke was clearly written on the faces of the smokers. Various ironic aspects of being a smoker struck me with great force in that moment.

The first was that the reason that it took so long to light up after the meal was that no one wanted to be the first to do so. So whilst the non-smokers were chatting and relaxing, the smokers were tense, waiting for someone else to light up, fighting with themselves, desperate to prove, "I'm not the weakest smoker here, I'm not going to be the first to light up. It would be terrible if I were the only smoker." So during that ten minutes the smokers were not able to relax and enjoy the after dinner chat. They were a lot less happy and more stressed than the non-smokers. However, the smokers didn't see it like that. Many probably felt pleased, even had a sense of satisfaction at not being the first to light up, for not being the 'weakest'. The suffering had been turned by the twisted reasoning of addiction into a hollow victory over the other smokers, or at least over the one who lit up first: "At least I'm not as badly hooked as him!" However, from my point of view as a non-smoker and former smoker, I saw only the slavery and the suffering of being a smoker.

If you ever find yourself in a similar situation where smokers are permitted to smoke at the table after a meal, you will see that they are not happier than non-smokers; they don't have an extra pleasure. It is simply that a smoker cannot feel normal, relaxed and happy if he cannot smoke. In fact, he can become irritable and miserable very quickly. What is clear from watching smokers at meals is that the eating actually interferes with their smoking. Whilst I was a smoker, I was often in a rush at the end of a meal to dash off and smoke. I can distinctly remember the irritation I felt if I got stuck with a slow eater and how I would transmit my impatience one way or another

Where is the pleasure in that? Like any addict, the smoker sees things the opposite to how they really are. He has lived all of his life with the emptiness caused by nicotine withdrawal. He doesn't see that each time he smokes he is just relieving the nicotine withdrawal caused by the previous cigarette. He doesn't understand why; it's just that he feels better when he smokes. He is like a goldfish which has no concept of water. The goldfish doesn't know what water is because it's always been there. It's invisible to him.

Although I am not in favour of the blunt instrument of prohibition and punishment (education might be more complicated but far more effective), now that smokers in many countries have to step outside, perhaps into the cold or rain to smoke, ever more are realising that smoking is not a pleasure but an obligation, a type of slavery. The tobacco industry, like the worst slave owners of old, doesn't care if you die, suffer horrible diseases or just suffer a crap quality of life, as long as you keep buying cigarettes.

Some smokers justify smoking as having some social benefit. Perhaps this argument had some dubious merit when you were fifteen! (The reality is that any youngster who is able to resist social pressure and stand up for himself and refuse to smoke, is far more likely to earn the respect of his peers – something that the more insecure adolescent does not see.) The opposite is true today. In order to smoke, you have to leave the table, your fellow diners, the conversation, the warmth of companionship and stand outside to smoke, which to my mind, however you look at it, simply isn't social. Smokers do not enjoy smoking after a meal; it is just that they can't feel as happy or as relaxed as a non-smoker if they can't smoke. I ask you again: Where is the pleasure in that?

Have you noticed that the cigarettes that seem to be the most pleasurable are the ones that you smoke when you've had to wait? The longer you have to wait, the better it seems. Why is that? After all, cigarettes are disgusting, smelly and toxic. The prize is not the cigarette; it never was. Smokers smoke to relieve the irritation of nicotine withdrawal and the longer you wait, the more you appreciate the relief. Rather like not eating for a long time, the longer you've waited, the better it seems when you do finally eat. Everyone has their favourite foods to relieve hunger but if you're hungry enough, you become less choosy about what you will or won't eat. The big difference is that food is something that we need to survive; it's vital fuel and maintenance material. Nicotine and the thousands of chemical compounds in a cigarette are highly toxic and poisonous. You only feel better when you smoke a cigarette because the previous cigarette made you feel worse.

What about concentration? For all of my smoking life and in the nineties, when I first started working with smokers in Spain, smoking was permitted almost everywhere. Many smokers were convinced that they could not concentrate without a cigarette, simply because they never had to. The idea of concentration or creativity without a cigarette was enough to make many break out in a cold sweat. Why should that be? The reason is simple. To be able to concentrate on any difficult task, one first has to remove as many distractions as possible. A smoker has the constant distraction of his body craving nicotine. A common sight nowadays outside companies is the smoker pacing up and down whilst talking on his mobile. Apart from transmitting the message to his boss: "I may be outside smoking but look, I am working," when he lights his cigarette he can concentrate better than a moment ago but in reality, even whilst smoking he simply cannot concentrate as well as if he were a non-smoker because, even with his cigarette lit, he manages to only partially relieve the withdrawal. Apart from this, when you smoke you cannot help but reduce the oxygen available to your brain, which clearly reduces your capacity to concentrate.

Some years ago a woman, a professional artist, came to a session. She smoked at least two packs a day. During the session she kept repeating, "I want to stop smoking but how am I going to be able to work without a cigarette? Smoking for me is a part of my creative process. I don't know if I can be creative or concentrate without smoking." She was clearly worried about this but had been diagnosed with the first symptoms of emphysema. Some three months after the session she telephoned to say that she was absolutely delighted to be free of her nicotine addiction. Furthermore, she explained that she felt more creative, more energetic and more able to concentrate than when she smoked. "I simply don't understand how on earth I was able to work as a smoker. I wasted so much time and energy smoking, all because I believed that I couldn't work without a cigarette – amazing, because in reality the opposite is true. I work so much better now." She expressed a very important point about smoking and drug addiction in general: what we believe whilst we are addicted is usually the opposite to reality.

As the artist above explained, smoking doesn't help you concentrate. Think of the typical situation of watching a film in the cinema or attending a presentation where smoking is prohibited. Before entering, a smoker will smoke what he or she calculates as necessary to get through the presentation – maybe just one, maybe two or three. Now, should the film or presentation go on for much longer than anticipated then irritation quickly sets in. The smoker cannot concentrate as he is wondering if and when he'll be able to smoke a cigarette. Let's imagine now that the smoker manages to sneak out and smoke a cigarette. He'll come back feeling more able to concentrate. So in his mind the cigarette has helped him concentrate. The reality is the opposite; it was the cigarette which stopped him from concentrating in the first place and even once he's smoked, he still will not be able to concentrate as well as if he were a non-smoker. As always, the smoker's view is the opposite to reality. This is not surprising as just like the eagle in the Taoist story, he simply knows no better. The smoker has lived with the withdrawal, the constant craving and distraction all of his adult life. It's 'normal'; it's invisible. He doesn't see the reality: that all he gets from a cigarette is partial relief of the withdrawal symptoms caused by the previous cigarette.

The tobacco industry thrives on this confusion and will reinforce the idea whenever possible. In the 70's and 80's tobacco advertising in magazines often boasted that their particular brand of cigarette gave 'full satisfaction'. Think, something can only satisfy if there is a pre-existing condition of dissatisfaction. What might be the cause of the pre-existing dissatisfaction? Nicotine withdrawal of course! The smoker smokes to try and relieve the sense of dissatisfaction caused by the previous cigarette. There is nothing to give up, absolutely nothing to sacrifice.

Whenever a smoker thinks of stopping smoking what usually springs to mind are those situations impossible to imagine without a cigarette. Many smokers at some time in the session will declare what for them is their 'acid test': "If tomorrow morning I can drink my coffee without smoking a cigarette then I will know that I am really a non-smoker." However, the all-time number one favourite is: "I can imagine many situations without a cigarette but I find it so hard to imagine a drink without a cigarette. If this weekend, when I'm out with my smoking friends, I can spend the entire night with them and not smoke, then I'll know that I'm truly a non-smoker."

Whilst the mechanics of addiction are the same in all smokers, each person is, as they say, 'a world unto himself'. A nervous person believes that he smokes to calm his nerves. Others might feel that they smoke to help them concentrate. Some only smoke during the week to cope with work-related stress, whilst others smoke only at weekends when they feel they have no stress. It really is fascinating how in the same session, many will claim to smoke for diametrically opposite motives and effects, whilst often the same smoker will claim diametrically opposed effects at different times of the day. Either nicotine is a truly miraculous drug that should make smokers immediately identifiable (I'm not referring here that they tend to smell like giant ashtrays and have less energy), I mean that if nicotine really did all that the tobacco industry and their PR henchmen would have us believe, then smokers would be quickly identifiable, as they would always look smugly satisfied, never shows signs of stress, possess superhuman powers of concentration, never be bored and of course look unbelievably cool. Know any smoker that fits that description? Me neither! There simply are no genuine benefits to smoking, not one; there is nothing to give up.

Let's take as our next example, social cigarettes. When we go out, above all during the weekend to a bar or a party, our objective is to enjoy ourselves, which means feeling that we are at 100% wellbeing. We put our work problems behind us; we've probably brushed our teeth, showered and smell divine. We've also eaten enough and we are dressed in clothes that we know make us utterly irresistible. So before we even step out, we have eliminated most of the potential drags on our wellbeing. You find yourself at your favourite night spot, good music, comfortable surroundings, attentive waiters. You are surrounded by friends who love you. Once you've done all that, you'll be at 100% wellbeing right? Well, there is a chance of that if you don't smoke. If you smoke however, you'll have that niggling nicotine withdrawal feeling and so you'll light a cigarette. It will seem very special. Why? Because it's a very special moment for non-smokers too; they too have left their problems behind; they have been through the same process and there is every chance that they are enjoying 100% wellbeing. So would the smoker if he didn't still have that niggling feeling of nicotine withdrawal. When you light a cigarette it really does seem one of the better ones – special. But the moment was special anyway and even whilst smoking your cigarette, your level of tolerance means you still cannot get rid of all of the nicotine withdrawal. Of course one is not enough and you soon light another and another. In fact, in a very short time you're not even smoking consciously; you're smoking automatically. The act of putting out and lighting each cigarette is now automatic. What is really happening is that although you cannot get to 100%, deep down, there is a kind of slight, panicky feeling that you have to keep smoking just to stay happy.

What complicates the social situation is the introduction of alcohol into the equation. Many smokers wrongly believe that there is some psychological connection between alcohol and tobacco: that drinking makes you smoke. It doesn't. There are many non-smokers or ex-smokers who manage perfectly well to drink alcohol and enjoy themselves without smoking. Alcohol acts to lessen or remove inhibitions, so you no longer try to exert any control. A smoker who has stopped smoking with a sense of sacrifice will spend his life trying to resist the temptation to smoke, perhaps with some success. However, once he has ingested sufficient alcohol, his inhibitions disappear.

Alcohol can only uncover a pre-existing desire to smoke; it does not create the desire.

Alcohol also acts as an anaesthetic. The smoker is out to enjoy himself and just for the night, sod the consequences. As I wrote earlier, smokers smoke what their bodies will tolerate. The anaesthetic effect of the alcohol means that you can smoke more without feeling the effects until the following day. A common experience for many smokers, after

68

going on a bender on Saturday night and smoking twice as much they would normally smoke, is that they are unable to smoke during most of Sunday, not because they are endowed with bigger 'cojones' on Sundays (that is to say they are stronger-willed on Sundays) but because they are so saturated with all the toxins in the cigarette, that the very idea of smoking a cigarette provokes a sense of nausea. Just watch smokers in those social situations. They don't enjoy each cigarette. They're smoking automatically; they don't even realise that they're smoking. There is just the compulsion, the desire to maintain their impaired level of wellbeing. Of course this situation can quickly change if they run low on cigarettes or they cannot smoke; then they quickly become irritable, uncomfortable and bad-tempered. Smoking cannot make you happy; you cannot even feel as comfortable as a non-smoker but if you cannot smoke, the evening is very quickly ruined.

As children we were manipulated into believing that smoking would make us more attractive, sexier, braver, cooler etc. Once you're hooked, this message is reinforced to keep you hooked.

Smokers are constantly manipulated to believe that, although smoking is dangerous, there are genuine benefits to be had. So long as you continue to believe the lie that the cigarette provides a genuine pleasure, helps you relax, concentrate, etc., then, whenever you try to stop smoking, you will feel that you are being forced to sacrifice something. It is also used to confirm (especially to youngsters) that it is cool, edgy etc. The idea of never being able to smoke another cigarette (not even one, sob, sob) will leave you feeling deprived. Your attitude will be, "I want to smoke (just one) but I can't even smoke that. It's not fair!" See these beliefs for what they are: cynical manipulation of your mental map. The truth is that there is nothing to give up or sacrifice.

We have discussed the manipulation that creates a sense of sacrifice. However, there is also manipulation designed to stop you from even trying to stop smoking. This second type of manipulation is what I call 'electric fence brainwashing'. Let me explain... In Cantabria where I live there are many horses, often kept within the bounds of their fields with an electric fence. If you're not familiar with them, an electric fence is usually made of a plastic tape into which fine wires are woven to conduct electricity. Once connected, the fence will give a fierce electric shock to whatever animal (horses and humans alike) that touches it. The shock is not dangerous but one shock is generally all that a horse needs to dissuade him from trying to escape. Once a horse has learnt this, farmers being a thrifty lot, will often disconnect the electricity. The horse will not try to cross the fence. Think about it! A 500 kilo horse fenced in by nothing more than an idea, a belief. There are striking similarities between these horses and smokers. The smoker is in a similar situation. The only thing that keeps him trapped are his beliefs – nothing more. This is the mental manipulation which goes something like this:

- *It is almost impossible to stop smoking.*
- *In order to stop, you are going to have to suffer (a lot).*
- *It will probably change your character for the worse.*
- *You will almost certainly get fat.*
- *You can never be free.*
- *You will always miss them.*
- *Once a smoker always a smoker.*
- *Even after all of that suffering, you will almost certainly start smoking again.*
- *All your suffering will have been for nothing.*

Let's imagine that we aren't talking about stopping smoking. I think that you'll agree that to start any project with a set of beliefs similar to those above, reduces your chances of success to almost zero. I don't need to tell you what project, because it is clear that these beliefs will create an attitude of hopeless pessimism that will doom any project to failure. In fact, if you believe all of the above, you probably wouldn't even bother to try to stop smoking. It is a testament to the intelligence and bravery of many smokers that, in spite of the 'electric fence', many do try and succeed in freeing themselves. See the manipulated mental model for what it is: nothing more than an imaginary barrier that you have been conditioned to perceive in a certain way and to fear.

When a smoker tries to stop smoking, it is his belief that he will fail that creates the failure, not the failure which creates the belief. However, he will use his experience of the failure to reinforce his pre-existing belief.

These beliefs are based on the mental models that have been driven into us without us even realising it, rather like the parasite which manipulates the behaviour of his host, the ant. There is nothing in it for the ant except a rather unpleasant death. (Sounds like smoking to me.) The danger is that we don't see these parasitic ideas for what they are: brainwashing, manipulation of our mental models in order to enrich people, organisations and companies for whom – contrary to what their titles and their marketing suggest – our wellbeing is not of the least importance.

7

Monkey see, monkey do

Other smokers are often the tobacco industry's best salesmen. The saddest aspect of this is that they pay to be salesmen. They pay not only in cash, but also with their quality of life, energy, vitality, freedom and self-respect.

For many of us, our childhoods were full of parents, uncles, aunts and grandparents who smoked. Many told you, with a cigarette in their hand, "Whatever you do, don't start smoking." The fact is that they all wish they'd never started in the first place. However, actions make more of an impression than words. Your uncle Eric might tell you a hundred times that smoking is bad and dangerous, but when you see him taking a deep drag after a meal, wearing that look of satisfaction on his face, then it's clear to you that Uncle Eric is getting something out of it. You cannot see in that moment that he is a nicotine addict. Prohibiting it only makes it more attractive.

Tobacco companies recognise the power of prohibition to make something more attractive to adolescents. Marlboro (yes, those scumbags again) made a big media offensive a while back about not encouraging adolescents to smoke. What they did was to put various warnings on cigarette packs which consisted in messages such as: 'If you are a minor, you are forbidden to smoke', 'Smoking for adults only'. In Spain they have now settled on 'Prohibida la venta a menores de 18 años.' (Sale prohibited to minors under-18.) Can you imagine a better way to make smoking desirable to an insecure adolescent? What did the government do about this? Or NGO's like the national Cancer Association? Nothing! Why not? Possible reasons include that they are idiots who were unable to understand that it was no more than a cynical effort by Marlboro to hook youngsters. Perhaps they are more interested in themselves, their own careers and benefits. (I at no time refer to volunteers in these organisations who are wonderful and well-meaning people). One only has to look at the pathetic way in which the smoking ban of 2006 was implemented in Spain. "What smoking ban?" said visitors to Spain. If you didn't know one existed then it would have been impossible to tell from the behaviour of smokers who faced little or no restrictions in most bars, restaurants, pubs, and public places. In Madrid we even had the spectacle of the president of the community rolling back the few restrictions that were made (remember simply to protect the health of non-smokers who do not want to smoke either passively or actively). I wonder how many people are now sick, how many youngsters are now addicted thanks to her corrupting influence? A direct result of her cynical meddling was that state-run companies that had previously removed smoking from all public areas, reintroduced smoking (both active and passive) into the most important communal area, the cafeteria. Many non-smokers simply stopped using it.

The use of smoking role models is also effective, be it the hero or better still, the anti (establishment)-hero. A certain film targeting insecure adolescent boys fizzing with testosterone, starring Vin Diesel, springs to mind. The character he plays is a tough macho half-wit who smokes constantly. Vin Diesel smokes so much in this film in fact that one could be forgiven for believing that the film is about smoking and that the adventures he has, incidental.

In Spain we also have the 'I smoke because I'm an intellectual' sell which remains remarkably popular. For many years, certain writers have used the cigarette as a rather silly prop. They present their smoking as somehow being part of the credentials of an intellectual. It fits in with the rather pretentious 'tortured soul' school of creativity. Just the other day my wife received her monthly magazine from her book club. The magazine often carries a picture of a writer alongside the book they wish to promote. On various occasions the edition features a picture of an 'intellectual' Spanish author. These pictures are clearly posed and the author often holds a lighted cigarette in his hand whilst wearing what he believes to be an 'intellectual' expression. (In fact it makes him look an utter pillock.) We are talking here not just of vanity but vanity in one of its saddest forms. Is the man so insecure that he needs a cigarette to reassure himself and others that he is, in fact, a genuine intellectual? It's sad. Wherever you go, you will find either well-meaning smokers who try to persuade you that you must not smoke or the plonker in whose mind the cigarette marks him or her out as something special. Well the news is that it does mark them out as special but not in the way they had hoped.

Many clients come to our sessions, worrying about how they will deal or face up to smokers after they have stopped smoking. However, once they stop, they usually find that observing smokers, far from tempting them, helps to reinforce their decision.

All smokers want to stop smoking and at the same time all would like to keep on smoking (at least a few special ones). Whatever the addiction, there is always a kind of complicity between addicts. All addicts know instinctively (and often consciously) that they are doing something stupid. Smokers are no exception. A lone smoker in the company of non-smokers feels uncomfortable and slightly absurd but in the company of other smokers, experiences a kind of kinship; it's a relief not to feel stupid. They indulge in group rationalization, talking of such things as the unfairness of smoking bans, whining about their right to smoke. I couldn't agree more; smokers have the right to keep on smoking but they miss the point: smoking bans do not stop smokers from smoking; they just allow people who don't want to smoke from being forced to do so. The desire and right to not breathe something foul and carcinogenic if we don't want to, would normally be respected, right? Although all human beings fart, farting at the dinner table is understandably considered bad manners. Imagine dining with a person who insists that they simply cannot enjoy a meal unless they are allowed to fart between courses; or that a coffee simply doesn't taste the same if they cannot fart at the same time. Whilst we accept farting as normal, that it is indeed human to fart, we would not behave in that way or accept another behaving in that way at the dinner table or in any other social setting. Now, imagine someone insisting not only that they needed to fart at the table but what's more, accuses you of being inconsiderate or intolerant because you don't want to breath his farts. Unlike second-hand smoke, farts are not generally carcinogenic.

Another common rationalization (one that I firmly held whilst I smoked) is that those who don't smoke are clearly miserable swine who don't know how to 'enjoy' themselves. Smokers might compare notes of unpleasant encounters with rabid ex-smokers or evangelising non-smokers. These conversations could be accurately described as group rationalization sessions. Now you might say these conversations mean nothing. As a smoker, one of my first (unconscious) objectives, upon arriving at a party, was to identify and place myself next to the other smoker(s). I felt more comfortable with a fellow addict. This does not happen with anything else. For example, I love eating mangoes and am also bald but at parties I have no need or desire to seek out bald-headed mango-eaters in order to feel more comfortable. You see, neither being bald nor eating mangoes makes me feel stupid, thus I don't require reassurance.

This complicity cannot exist between smokers and ex-smokers. Imagine the following situation. A group of friends or colleagues smoke. They often reassure each other that it's OK to smoke. They manage to create a sense of "we might smoke but at least we know how to enjoy ourselves." So far so good – companionship through rationalisation. But what is the reality?

The reality is that smokers are bound together by their fear of stopping.

Now, imagine that one of the group stops smoking. He appears one day as a non-smoker. The smokers feel (secretly) envious, also uncomfortable and perhaps more than a bit betrayed. The previous conversations about the need to smoke, that fun people smoke, or that smoking isn't so bad, now seem a bit ludicrous. The complicity has evaporated. One or two in the group might even realise that they smoke out of fear. There is now perhaps talk in the group about stopping. There is very likely to be a smoker in the group, famous for being tight-fisted. Never in the collective memory of the group, has he been known to offer anyone a cigarette. Now all of a sudden he's there at the side of the ex-smoker, offering a cigarette in as casual a manner as possible, trying to tempt the ex-smoker back into the carcinogenic, foul-smelling nightmare. Some people have said that these smokers must be wicked. They are not; they just feel very uncomfortable, stupid and weaker than the ex-smoker. Their way of dealing with this is to drag others down as well.

There are two basic strategies for feeling good about yourself socially. One is to look for the best in people, to genuinely appreciate and feel happy for another person's good fortune, be accepting of one's own shortcomings and improve self-esteem by improving oneself. The second strategy is to find fault in others, to feel better about oneself by doing down or trashing others. Another person's success is seen as a threat rather than an inspiration. Unfortunately, the second category is more common. We are all capable of both types of behaviour. Addiction of any kind tends to reinforce the second posture.

Other smokers are, whether they are aware of it or not, salesmen for the tobacco industry. The saddest aspect is that they pay to be that. They pay with their hard-earned money, their health, their vitality, their peace of mind, their self-respect, their freedom and unfortunately in many cases with their lives.

8

Know thy enemy

We have spoken about how the massive mental manipulation gets us hooked and keeps us hooked. The whole criminal enterprise known as the tobacco industry assisted by Satan's mercenary little helpers (the PR industry) works on incremental improvement of percentages. If you have an industry worth billions, then improving the effectiveness of your product by just one or two percent (getting children hooked, keeping adults hooked, getting them to smoke more, corrupting law-makers, causing confusion in the minds of smokers and non-smokers alike), translates into millions in additional profits. This is precisely what the tobacco industry does. Millions are invested in incremental improvements in effectiveness. So now is a good time to know thy enemy. Perhaps I should start with an extract from an internal document from Philip Morris:

The cigarette should be conceived of not as a product but as a package. The product is nicotine. Think of the cigarette-pack as a storage container for a day's supply of nicotine... Think of the cigarette as the dispenser for a dose unit of nicotine... Smoke is beyond question the most optimised vehicle of nicotine delivery and the cigarette, the most optimised dispenser of smoke.' **(Philip Morris 1972)**

RJR too recognises it is in the drug business:

In a sense, the tobacco industry may be thought of as being a specialised, highly ritualised, and stylised segment of the pharmaceutical industry.' **(RJR 1972)**

There are currently within the EU some 600 additives authorized for inclusion in tobacco products. The regulation of these additives is so loose that only the tobacco companies can say which additives are in which cigarettes.

The myth is that the fantastic success of Marlboro as a world-leading global brand was the result of a powerful marketing campaign. This is not entirely true. The chemical manipulation history of the brand sheds some interesting light on the whole subject, with thanks to the Tobacco Institute:

Serious tobacco manipulation started in the late 1960's. Philip Morris (manufacturers of Marlboro) pioneered the manipulation techniques at a time when they were the smallest of America's six leading tobacco companies. By the middle of the seventies the tables had turned and Philip Morris had become the world's leading cigarette manufacturer, accounting for 20 percent of all cigarette sales and *more than 50% of sales to smokers 17 years old or younger.* Reverse engineering by competitors led other tobacco companies to the conclusion that this increase was due to 'ammonia technology'. When you add ammonia to nicotine, the uptake in the body of the smoker is increased. (Importantly, this uptake is increased in a way that could not be detected by the machines government laboratories used for determining the nicotine content of the cigarette.) What does this mean? The more nicotine that is absorbed, the more tolerant the body becomes; the more tolerant the body becomes, the smaller the relief; the smaller the relief, the more the smoker feels like smoking, and the more *he buys.* This sparked a race by other tobacco companies to master the manipulation of tobacco. Nowadays additives account for about 10% by weight of the cigarette.

Cigarette manipulation is now a cold-blooded and deadly science. It is a percentage game. Broadly speaking and based on the industry's own internal documentation, the action of these additives may be divided into the following categories:

1. Enhancers of the effect of nicotine. This includes the addition of such chemicals as ammonia and 'front-end loading' of the cigarette, both of which are designed to accelerate the impact of nicotine on the nervous system.
2. Sweeteners and chocolate make the cigarette more palatable to young users.
3. Additives such as cocoa and liquorice dilate the airways, allowing greater absorption of nicotine.
4. Substances to mask the smell and visibility of 'second-hand' smoke. This does nothing to reduce the toxicity of the smoke but attempts to disguise the fact that smoking is carcinogenic and impacts the cardiovascular system of passive smokers.
5. Analgesic additives which numb the throat to the aggravating effects of cigarette smoke. This amounts to a deliberate subversion of the body's defence mechanism.

6. Substances to mislead regulatory bodies regarding the nicotine and tar content of the cigarettes in tests.
7. Genetic manipulation of tobacco plants to increase nicotine content.

Some additives are toxic in their own right. Added to this, different additives when burned together, form new products of combustion which are themselves toxic. As I said at the beginning of this chapter, 'know thy enemy'.

Logically, these facts alone should be enough for anyone with at least half a brain to refrain from smoking but of course the mental manipulation and the fear it creates is so strong that whilst we smoke we prefer to close our minds to it. The reaction of Fernando, a smoking friend of mine, is typical. We were having a friendly chat about smoking and he asked me about the additives. I went through the list of the effects of ammonia, the bronchial dilators, the analgesics, the cynical manipulation. None of the points elicited a reaction until I explained how the flavour is manipulated to make the product more attractive to children. That was the point he interrupted me to say, "that is serious."

To try and get a perspective on the incongruity of his reaction, let us imagine for a moment that we are not talking about tobacco but about cheese. Just imagine the horror you would feel to find out that cheese manufacturers were manipulating cheese, using toxic additives to make it addictive. What is more, that when cooked cheese produces additional toxic, carcinogenic compounds that would normally be rejected by your body but to combat this, the cheese-makers add chemicals which prevent your body from recognising that it is being poisoned. Furthermore, you discover to your horror that about half the people eating cheese will die a horrible 'cheese-related' death. What would your reaction be to this horrific news? You would simply stop eating cheese, right? Even if the cheese industry produced a slightly less toxic version (lite), you still wouldn't feel tempted to eat 'lite cheese' would you?

So why do we not react in the same way with tobacco. Simple, it is the fear that nicotine addiction produces; the idea that we cannot face life without the support of a cigarette or the idea that life will somehow cease to be enjoyable without a cigarette. The irony of this is that we had to work so hard to get ourselves hooked in the first place just to overcome the horrible smell and taste, the coughing, the dizziness and the vomiting. Our experience of smoking is truly awful and yet a few years later we become anxious when we get low on cigarettes. My question to you is: so what has changed? The drug hasn't changed; it's exactly the same drug as it was years ago; only our perception of it changes.

Apathy, Corruption and Self-interest

The efforts of the tobacco industry would be futile if they were not aided and abetted by the very people and organisations that are there, supposedly to protect us. Not so long ago during a stop-smoking session, a man became quite indignant. He said, "Surely if what you are saying is true, why doesn't the government do something about it?" The man would not have asked that question if he had been aware of the Golden Rule. Remember:

He who has the gold makes the rules.

The taxes on tobacco and alcohol are very important sources of income for the government. What is more, they are soft sources of income. For example, if the government were to increase income tax by 1%, there would be an uproar, even demonstrations on the streets. However, increasing tobacco taxes by 10 or 15% provokes a moan from smokers and little else. Smokers feel that they 'need' their drug and some feel secretly that maybe the price increase will help them stop. In a perverse sort of way others feel that they deserve it. A tactic of the tobacco industry if you cannot win (also used effectively by other big industries), is to at least muddy the waters as much as possible. Industry sponsored investigations are cynically touted as scientific studies (in reality no more than PR and marketing) and are commissioned to put into doubt such aspects as the danger of second-hand smoke, or to show the 'positive' impact of sponsorship, or how advertising isn't to get children to smoke but just to get smokers to change brands, or to demonstrate that smokers are an economic benefit to society. The argument goes like this: smokers pay additional taxes, they tend not to survive to old age and thus cost society less. Therefore, the overall economic effect is positive. These are usually cold-hearted, cynical and heartless initiatives thought up by Satan's little helpers, the ubiquitous PR industry. Apart from being of questionable validity (there are studies which also show the opposite), scientific studies, (above all where Big Tobacco, Big Alcohol, Big Pharma, Big Food, and lately Big Oil are involved) are increasingly meaningless, as in reality many of these studies are marketing by another name. Big industry money is used directly and indirectly to influence, corrupt, and browbeat supposedly independent scientists, doctors and government bureaucrats. It is a sad reflection on our society that whether something is worth doing or not, is increasingly determined by the short-term economic benefit. No account is taken of the suffering involved, the lack of wellbeing, the fear, the inability of the smoker to realise his full potential. These effects are much more harmful to the individual and to society as a whole in the long term.

Traditionally, scientific studies are considered scientific once they are peer-reviewed, that is to say reviewed by other *independent* scientists and/or doctors and published in a recognised journal. Until quite recently a vital requirement of such reviews was that the scientists or doctors responsible for reviewing the study had to demonstrate their independence of whatever industry might be affected by the study. This requirement has now been dropped by the world's leading medical journals. Why? Quite simply because there are hardly any independent scientists or doctors left. It has simply become too difficult to find scientists or doctors who are sufficiently independent, that is to say who have not received money from the industries whose studies they are supposed to be reviewing. Too many scientists and doctors have benefited materially from these industries and to exclude those who have, would mean there simply wouldn't be enough left over to undertake the reviews!

After the tobacco industry, the industry which benefits most from the smoker is the pharmaceutical industry. They have made an absolute fortune selling ineffective treatments which, according to many truly **independent** studies, reduce your chances of stopping smoking. (I refer you again to Reference 1.) The fact is that 90% of smokers who stop smoking successfully and remain stopped after one year, do so without taking any sort of substitute or medication.

The latest scam is the sale of electronic cigarettes. If you are a nicotine addict then the pharmaceutical industry wants to be your preferred supplier. They don't want you to stop smoking; they want to sell you *their* drugs. They use their immense financial muscle to subvert NGOs, national associations and not-so-independent experts in order to sell their product. They are in the business of creating cosy little clubs which often include members of the medical profession to protect their joint interests. I once asked a doctor friend of mine just how effective were the medicines that he prescribed. He answered that he had no idea as to the effectiveness of most of the drugs he prescribed, as practically all of his information came from the manufacturers of these drugs or bodies financed by them.

The problem with nicotine addiction is the same as for any other addiction; it is primarily psychological. It is the way in which you perceive the drug. You cannot change what someone believes with a pill.

However, we are so asleep that we accept quasi-scientific explanations which sound plausible, but in reality are no more than a kind of gobbledegook marketing. It is so desperately sad how so many people suffer unnecessarily because of our 'take-a-pill' mentality. A big problem for the medical profession is that they have a single (often not very effective) tool. Often, the only person that vouches for the efficiency of the tool is the salesman who sold it to them in the first place or one of his 'pals'. I repeat the words of Maslow: 'If your only tool is a hammer then all of your problems start to look like nails.'

Quite often a client who has understood all of the arguments, will say something like, "If only I knew then what I know now, I would never have started smoking. Nobody told us about smoking being a drug addiction; it was just a habit but kids nowadays simply aren't exposed to that same manipulation either in the cinema or on the TV. They are told very early on at school that it is drug addiction and that it's dangerous. And yet they still start smoking."

We live in a culture which mindlessly worships celebrity. Youngsters want to emulate the famous. We idolise not the great thinkers and scientists, writers or spiritual leaders, but instead far too much importance is attached to the often superficial opinions of actors, singers and celebrities, many of whom lead shallow, drug-dependent and amoral lives. Many youngsters, when questioned about what they want to do with their lives, reply, "I want to be famous," and when asked for what, the reply is "I don't mind, I just want to be famous." Here is a bit more from the US Tobacco Institute:

Photographs of actors, actresses and models with cigarette in hand have become increasingly common during the 1990's. Whether intended to convey rebellion, risk-taking and defiance, to evoke the movie-star glamour of the 1940s and 1950s, or simply to shock the audience, the cigarette has been included as an accessory on the catwalk, in fashion features and in clothing advertisements directed to the young. Marlboro's image is enhanced by being the brand publicly smoked by American model and actress, Jerry Hall.

Here is a quote from Hamish Maxwell of Philip Morris Companies:

'Smoking is being positioned as an unfashionable, as well as unhealthy, custom. We must use every creative means at our disposal to reverse this destructive trend. I do feel heartened at the increasing number of occasions when I go to a movie and see a pack of cigarettes in the hands of the leading lady. This is in sharp contrast to the state of affairs just a few years ago, when cigarettes rarely showed up on camera. We must

continue to exploit new opportunities to get cigarettes on screen and into the hands of smokers.'

Something more about Philip Morris:

In August 2006, federal judge Gladys Kessler ruled that Philip Morris USA, together with other tobacco companies, violated racketeering laws by creating a massive illegal enterprise to defraud the American people — and that this enterprise continues. The large-scale fraud described in the legal ruling includes PM USA's denials that it marketed to youth.

The same Philip Morris USA is now running ads urging Hollywood to leave its brands out of movies but has also run ads questioning whether second-hand smoke causes lung cancer. The present ads are signed 'Youth Smoking Prevention', a registered trademark of Philip Morris USA. According to a published study, this same campaign's television spots actually make teens who view them **more likely to smoke.**

This cynical mental manipulation permeates all levels and aspects of our society. Governments do little to combat it. Even some non-smokers believe it. For example, it isn't unusual to see non-smokers at weddings smoking the free cigarettes and cigars. It is obvious from the kack-handed way they smoke that they are non-smokers. They don't like it but they will do it because it is 'sophisticated', because it's what people do to celebrate. There exists in these situations a social pressure to smoke.

Although you are most likely to get hooked during adolescence (a lot of the effort by the tobacco industry targets this group), I often see smokers in our sessions who sadly got hooked later in life. For example, some people start at university because of the illusion that smoking helps relieve stress and improves concentration. They quickly become hooked and discover that rather than improve concentration, they rapidly reach a point where they can't concentrate without a cigarette.

One of the most extreme cases I ever saw of this was a 47 year old executive who was tasked with restructuring a company. It was a very stressful time. He was the only non-smoker on a team of six managers. He asked why they all smoked and they answered that it helped them with stress. He thought, "Well, I feel stressed; maybe smoking can help me through these next few months of stress – it seems to work for the others." When I met the man he had already spent two years smoking two packs a day.

Never underestimate just how cold-blooded and evil the people running the tobacco industry really are. One of the reasons they get away with their dirty games is the fact that most people simply cannot believe

81

just how evil they really are. For example, in Australia some years ago Marlboro made a big hoo-ha about how they do not and would not target children for tobacco sales. At the same time, as part of a promotion, they gave away with each pack of twenty a sequined purse (the sort that only an adolescent girl might find attractive). Can you imagine how these people work? They have to think of ways to get children hooked to a drug that will ruin the quality of their lives and probably shorten it. Can you imagine working in PR for the tobacco industry, dedicating day after day of your life figuring out how to lie to people in order to make money out of making them sick. Well that's what they do. I truly don't know whether there is such a thing as Karma but if there is, these people will surely come back as dung beetles. Even that would be better than they deserve.

9

But what about just one or an occasional cigarette?

First of all, you the reader cannot smoke just a few cigarettes. If you could then you would not be reading this book. I always ask in the session if anyone has tried to cut down. Everyone has. Their experience is that it is a kind of torture. It becomes their obsession.

There are just two factors which determine the number of cigarettes that a smoker habitually smokes. The first is the physical capacity of the smoker to withstand the systematic poisoning of his own body. The second is opportunity. There are no more factors. Most people wrongly believe that the more you smoke, the more addicted you are; that the more a smoker smokes, the greater his addiction. You even hear doctors and psychologists authoritatively using terms like 'heavily addicted'. It is such utter claptrap. You cannot tell how addicted a smoker is simply by counting the number of cigarettes he smokes. The fact is that smokers will always smoke all that their bodies can stand, provided they have the opportunity to do so.

Your body has three basic lines of defence against poisoning:

a) The first is a 'poison alert'. Anything that tastes horrible or produces an unpleasant reaction when you first try it is probably poisonous. In other words — horrible taste, dizziness, coughing, vomiting mean, "Don't do it. It's poison!"

b) The second is metabolising the drug into a less toxic substance (in the case of nicotine the metabolite is cotinine) and then eliminating it through urine, faeces and sweat.

c) The third is tolerance. If you insist on carrying on, your body will develop a tolerance to the drug. What this means essentially, is that a fixed dosage of the drug has an ever-decreasing effect.

Often in the sessions we have smokers who smoke just three or five cigarettes a day. They book and attend the session like any other smoker. When they share this information with the rest of the group, a heavy smoker who smokes say thirty or more a day, will often ask, "What the hell are you doing here then? I dream of being able to smoke just five a day. I'd pay to smoke 5 cigarettes a day." The 'heavy smoker' mistakenly believes that anyone who smokes five a day must be happy with it. What we quickly discover is that all the smokers in the session (unless they're trying to cut down) smoke what their bodies can take, provided that they have the opportunity to do so. They are in the session because they are equally addicted.

Some smokers start to feel unwell if they smoke more than five in a day; others need to smoke twenty to reach the same point; others forty. The quantity they smoke says nothing about their level of addiction.

The fact is all smokers smoke what they can, as long as they have the opportunity to do so. Many smokers feel that if they could just control themselves and smoke just 3 or 5 a day, they would be happy. It is not possible to do this without sooner or later smoking as much, if not more than before.

Smoking is a drug addiction. This means that your body will keep on developing a tolerance to the drug and that you have to take bigger and bigger doses of nicotine for an ever diminishing sense of relief. You eventually reach a point where you cannot increase the dose any further because your body simply cannot stand it. At this point you suffer constant withdrawal.

For most smokers, cutting down is what they do when they fail to stop completely. They stop a while and start thinking things like, "Just one puff won't do any harm," "I'll just smoke a cigar when I eat with friends Saturday nights," "It's got to be possible to keep it under control and just smoke five a day; it's just a question of getting used to it." There are four important problems here:

1. The smoker has stopped being a smoker who wants to be a non-smoker and has become an ex-smoker who wants to be an occasional smoker which is not possible because…

2. Your body becomes ever more tolerant to nicotine. If you choose to smoke five cigarettes day (that being the lowest limit you believe that you can live with), after a while the increased tolerance means that the relief you get from smoking those five cigarettes will be equivalent to smoking four cigarettes. Tolerance continues to increase, the relief continues to decrease. The smoker suffers a constant pressure to increase the dosage by smoking more, which is sad when you realise that…

3. The smoker is wishing for something that doesn't exist. The reason he wanted to stop smoking was that he didn't like being a smoker. If it were possible to smoke just a bit then he wouldn't have tried to stop completely in the first place. Remember, we all got hooked in the mistaken belief that we could smoke just a little. So the other mistake is the idea that...

4. If I smoke less then I will feel less hooked. If you've ever tried this, you will know that far from feeling less hooked, you end up thinking about nothing else. You find yourself constantly negotiating: "I'll finish this first, then I'll have a cigarette," or if you have decided to smoke every hour then it starts to seem that your watch is broken or at least slow.

The smoker now has created an unbearable situation. Even if he can apply strict discipline to smoke just five a day, sooner or later he steps over the line, possibly in a stressful situation or at a party. His consumption increases until he realises that he is now in the same place as before: firstly, wishing for something that doesn't exist (smoking just a bit) and feeling more hooked than ever.

Really understand this: smokers smoke all that they can. The essential tendency with any drug addiction is to do it compulsively and continuously. Smoking is no different.

For many smokers the cigarettes that are the most important are the cigarettes that they smoke first thing in the morning with a coffee. (For others, smoking too early makes them feel sick, so they have to wait.) As the day wears on, smoking becomes automatic and unconscious. The smoker might start to notice a bad taste in his mouth (which is why many smokers eat sweets and chew gum). Perhaps he starts to get a headache. Eventually, he reaches the point where he lights a cigarette but it tastes so horrible that after just a couple of puffs, he thinks, "Ugh! How disgusting!" and throws it away. Five minutes later he repeats the process and starts feeling absurd, asking himself, "If it tastes so horrible, why do I keep doing it?"

That is the process for a person who smokes forty cigarettes a day or for the person who smokes five a day. All smokers will exceed their limit at some point. Many a smoker will smoke two or three times more than usual at a party or on a Saturday night. On Sunday morning the smoker feels so sick that she cannot smoke a cigarette. She might try experimenting during the day to see whether or not it's possible to smoke but finds that they still taste foul. Then, perhaps at around five in the afternoon, things get back to normal and she can smoke at her usual rhythm. Often in a session a five-a-day smoker will say something like, "I normally smoke five a day except on Saturdays when I can smoke up to twelve but I feel so sick on Sunday that I don't smoke." Some smokers need to smoke two packs to reach that same saturated state. It has nothing to do with how addicted they are. The smoker who habitually smokes five and the smoker who habitually smokes thirty are addicted to the same degree. Given the opportunity, they will smoke all that their bodies can endure.

Smokers suffer all of this torture in exchange for what exactly? Nothing, not one single genuine benefit. Smoking is, always has been and always will be a sad, futile effort to relieve the withdrawal caused by the previous cigarette. There is nothing to sacrifice, nothing to give up. So what does smoking do for you?

10

Smoking makes you fearful

The most insidious and in my experience, the least talked about effect of smoking or any drug addiction is the way in which it gradually makes you more fearful, thereby undermining your courage and reducing your quality of life. None of us decided to become smokers all of our lives. We believed that we would never get hooked. In fact, many smokers who appear in our sessions started out as confirmed anti-smokers. They have suffered a smelly, choking childhood at the hands of their smoking parents, a house that always stank of dirty ashtrays, stuck in the car on long journeys with smoking parents, hating the smell and any thing to do with smoking. They wrongly believed that their parents smoked because weirdly, they enjoyed the taste and smell of burning tobacco. Thus, they easily fall into a treacherous mental model which goes like this: "If I hate smoking so much, then for sure I won't get hooked." Of course, what they don't realise is that the taste and smell have absolutely nothing to do with the addiction. If it did, nobody would ever smoke a second cigarette and nobody would ever become hooked.

However, the parasitic idea that was so successfully implanted during childhood now begins to take effect. The soon-to-be smoker starts smoking perhaps to fit in socially or because she believes that it will improve her concentration during her studies. With repeated exposure to the nicotine and the thousands of other toxic components in a cigarette, her tolerance increases and she finds herself smoking habitually and in steadily increasing quantities in social situations. She isn't conscious of why but she notices that she feels more comfortable with a cigarette. Remember that her mental model is: "I'll never get hooked." She therefore interprets all evidence through this prism, making it fit with the model. So instead of noticing the increase in her consumption, she notices the times when she doesn't smoke and uses this information to support her belief that she is still an occasional smoker, a social smoker.

We should never underestimate the capacity humans have for creative self-delusion, especially where addiction is concerned. In one extreme case during a session, a client suddenly interrupted me and said with an expression of amazement, "Fuck me! I still think of myself as an

occasional smoker. I've just realised that I actually smoke 25 to 30 a day!"
You might laugh or even feel relieved that at least you're not as deluded
as he is. But before you start feeling smug, ask yourself how often you
have misled yourself by keeping the real number of cigarettes that you
smoke deliberately vague: "I know I smoke more than a pack a day but
I've never really thought about how much more." How many times have
you lied to your doctor or your spouse about how many you smoke each
day?

After a failed attempt to stop or cut down, the cosy mental model
the smoker has constructed about being a social or occasional smoker,
starts to look a bit wobbly. In spite of her best efforts to keep things
vague, reality is now intruding. However, rather than coming right out
and saying, "I'm hooked," she starts an internal 'compensation' dialogue
which helps her feel more comfortable with the belief that she cannot
stop. The dialogue consists of thoughts such as: "I can stop whenever I
want but I don't want to right now," "Now's not the moment, I'll wait
until after the summer holidays, New Year," etc. Another compensation
dialogue now also starts: "Ok, I do smoke but I'm lucky because it
doesn't affect me." The tolerance to the drug nicotine grows and thus the
number of cigarettes smoked daily also grows. The tolerance increases to
a point where the smoker finds herself in a state of constant nicotine
withdrawal.

Once the nicotine withdrawal feeling becomes a permanent fixture
in our lives, we come to believe the opposite to reality: we come to
believe that it is life that creates this empty, insecure feeling and that the
cigarette, although toxic and foul smelling, removes it. If we cannot do
anything to relieve the feeling (smoke a cigarette), we quickly become
anxious, stressed and even panicky. As I wrote earlier, what we don't
realise is that…

*It is not the cigarette which relieves the feeling; it is the cigarette
which causes it. The empty feeling is the nicotine withdrawal.*

The panic that the smoker feels when he thinks about stopping
smoking is the feeling of having to live with that emptiness forever
without anything to help relieve it. But the cigarette doesn't relieve it; is
the cause of the empty feeling. What he believes and fears will happen if
he stops smoking is the opposite to reality. The empty feeling is the
nicotine withdrawal. One of the wonderful aspects of stopping smoking
is to be free of that constant, niggling, empty feeling and the anxiety,
stress, even panic that it engenders. The smoker not only experiences this
panic when he thinks about stopping smoking, also at any time he finds

himself short of cigarettes, or when he wants to but is not able to smoke, or when he's down to his last three cigarettes; or perhaps feels a mysterious pain in the chest, wheezes or sees spots in front of his eyes after a coughing fit. All of these things provoke fear: "I know I ought to stop but I don't know how," then smoking a cigarette to calm his nerves. The smoker finds himself feeling constantly fearful: fearful of the consequences of smoking if he carries on and fearful of not being able to smoke if he stops, but feels powerless to do anything about it. The irony of this is that it is nicotine which causes this fear. Non-smokers simply do not suffer any of these fears; they are caused by the cigarette.

The uncomfortable or even painful sensations and symptoms that we have all suffered with a headache or the flu, are much more intense than the empty feeling of nicotine withdrawal, yet do not cause panic. It is because we mistakenly called the empty feeling, "I want a cigarette," that it becomes imperative to smoke. Our lives become centred on avoiding, whenever possible, 'the empty feeling'. As our tolerance to the drug increases so does the frequency with which we seek relief and we find ourselves smoking ever more. We quickly get to a point where our life is planned according to the next opportunity to relieve the empty feeling (to smoke). Just watch smokers smoking compulsively before going into the cinema, or before going into the subway/underground. The "I want a cigarette" thought develops so that it is not just "I want a cigarette now" but "I have to make sure that I am *never* without them!" Any impediment to smoking, any possibility of finding ourselves without tobacco generates fear. We are guided constantly by the strength of this fear. Ironically we are not fearful of the *real* reality – that there is nothing to fear; being a non-smoker is marvellous. Sadly…

We become fearful of the feeling of fear.

The smoker feels less able to resist smoking. At some level he feels a constant fear: fear of not having enough tobacco, fear that smoking might kill him, fear that he is destroying his health, fear that he simply cannot manage without a cigarette. He spends time trying to avoid feeling fearful, trying to rationalize away his fear. The smoker really has little choice in the matter. If he had to consciously face the truth each time he lit a cigarette, he would be forced to think something like, "This addiction conditions absolutely every aspect of my life. This cigarette could be the one that kills me; it could provoke a horrible disease. This next cigarette will cost me at least 150,000 euros because if I smoke one, I'll have to smoke the next half a million." Like anything else in life, the more you practice, the better you become. By practicing avoiding fear you become a more fearful person.

The smoker gradually feels unable to handle difficult or stressful situations without a cigarette. Rather than say, "I cannot face this situation without a cigarette," he thinks, "The cigarette helps me," which is the opposite to what is really happening. ***He doesn't feel stronger with his cigarette; he just feels that he cannot cope without it.*** Prior to smoking, he could face any situation as he was; he didn't need anything extra. He is now a slave to his fear, a slave to the parasite and the tobacco industry.

Really get this clear: smokers believe that smoking somehow helps them; that smoking gives them courage, relaxes them. *It does the opposite.* Smokers need to smoke just to feel capable of doing things that non-smokers do without smoking. The cigarette does not make them braver or more relaxed − just the opposite. Apart from the constant discomfort of the withdrawal, the smoker always lives with constant fear and tension at some level. It is this fear that makes the life of the smoker smaller; even friendships are conditioned by the fear of not being able to smoke. You're not going to spend an evening at the house of a friend if smoking is not permitted, are you? This fear reduces the quality of life of the smoker. Fear conditions all aspects of life. I know of clients who refuse to take international flights, or have stopped going to the cinema because they cannot smoke. The most extreme example of this was a woman who won a holiday for two in Rome but wouldn't take the prize because of Italian smoking restrictions.

It is only when we stop smoking and experience the marvellous sense of freedom, the relief of not having to smoke that we come to realize just how much the fear had cowed us, how this fear of fear had conditioned every aspect of our lives. Many clients have commented on a marvellous sense of inner peace when they stop, as if a great weight had been taken off their backs, their lives no longer driven by fear. Many clients suddenly discover the courage to make changes in their lives that they knew they ought to make but couldn't find the courage to do so. One client in particular, telephoned some four months after stopping smoking to tell me that I should charge much more for our stop-smoking session. He said that since stopping smoking he had faced and overcome many problems in the restructuring of his business; problems, that whilst he smoked seemed 'too difficult' were now solved. He felt that the energy, clarity of thought and above all the courage he recovered, once he stopped smoking, were the key factors.

11

But at least before I had the illusion. Now I haven't even got that!

One of the daftest comments I hear goes something like this: "OK, I really understand that smoking gives me no genuine pleasure or help. I understand that all of these are illusions created by the chemical addiction and the mental manipulation. But before I came to see you at least I had those illusions to help me with my life. Now I don't even have these. You've taken them away!" Ideally, to achieve maximum effect, this last part should be delivered in a whiney tone of voice.

The first time I heard someone use this as a justification for starting smoking again, my initial feeling was that they were being purposely obtuse, deliberately misunderstanding me, looking to find a way around reality in order to justify carrying on smoking. It didn't take me long to realise the reason. The answer, as always, is fear: fear of having to face life without their consolation, companion, etc.

This is understandable to a point, not because smoking has any benefits; it doesn't, not even one, but just like the eagle-chick raised with chickens, we simply don't know any better. We did not choose to become smokers. Most of us were no more than children when we started. We have been smokers since adolescence. In other words, many of us have not experienced life as an adult non-smoker. In every stressful situation, every celebration, whenever we've had to concentrate, whenever we have been alone, the cigarette has accompanied us. The times that we wanted to smoke but weren't allowed to, or when we have run out of tobacco, have been stressful, anxious and panicky moments. Many smokers have never run out of tobacco for this very reason. Smokers, like all drug addicts, need to know where their next fix is coming from. When I smoked and came home from work, the thing that I always did, either on the way home or once I got there, was to make sure that I had *more than enough* cigarettes to last until the next day. This for me usually meant two packs. There was no way I was going to smoke them all but I needed them to feel secure. If I didn't have 'enough' cigarettes, which happened on a few occasions, I would take the car, drive to the local bar or garage and buy some. The need to have tobacco to hand is strong and common amongst smokers. Many city dwelling clients have described how they have gone down to the street in their pyjamas to buy tobacco at the nearest café. We simply feel that we cannot face life without a cigarette.

We become like Dumbo, the flying elephant in Disney's animated film. For those readers who haven't seen Dumbo, it is very American and very Disney. The plot can be summed up like this: the cute and adorable underdog, after much suffering, faces his fears, realizes that they are not real and never were, realizes that he is enough and wins the day.

Dumbo is a lovable, cute (remember this is Disney) little circus elephant. He suffers years of bullying by all the other elephants in the circus because of his unusually large ears. However, Dumbo is very special. Why? He can fly! (His ears are so big, they can serve as wings.) With the help of some friends, he learns to fly. In spite of all the proof to the contrary, Dumbo simply cannot believe that his ability to fly is natural. He comes to believe that he can fly only when he holds a magic feather in his trunk. Now, because he cannot remember being able to fly without the feather in his trunk, he mistakenly believes he simply cannot fly *unless* he has the magic feather held in his trunk. Of course, all of us watching the film know that Dumbo can really fly all by himself. We all know that he is enough. We also know that his feather isn't magic at all. It is his belief that the feather has magic properties and the fear that this creates when he tries to imagine flying without it, that causes the problem. He doesn't believe in himself; he's always been the underdog and knows no other life.

When I am talking to smokers I sometimes feel like a child once again, sitting in the darkened cinema with an almost unbearable desire to shout out to Dumbo, "You don't need the feather, it does nothing for you; it's an illusion. Let go of it and you'll discover what a great guy you really are." I get a similar feeling when I talk to smokers in this situation. They have lived all of their adult lives with a cigarette, believing that cigarettes help them in some way, afraid that without them they simply won't be able to function.

Like Dumbo they are confusing cause and effect. Dumbo was afraid to fly without the feather, not because the feather was magic but because **he believed** that the feather was magic. In the same way, the smoker is frightened to face life without a cigarette, not because the cigarette does anything for him, he just believes that it does. There are two big differences between Dumbo and the smoker.

Why did you start smoking again?

The first is that the feather is not addictive, is not toxic, does not cause horrific illness, does not cost a fortune, nor make Dumbo smell like a giant ashtray; doesn't leave him feeling constantly tired and short of breath. The second difference is that once Dumbo realises that the feather does nothing for him, he becomes a happy, little elephant from that moment on and forever. He spends the rest of his day flying around doing aerobatics, celebrating his ability and generally enjoying life. What a berk Dumbo would have been if he realised that he didn't need the feather to fly and had started to whine, "I know the feather is an illusion, that I can fly without it but at least before I had the illusion that I needed a feather to fly!" It simply wouldn't make sense, would it? However, that is precisely what many smokers do who try to stop *por cojones*. Instead of celebrating and saying, "Brilliant, I'm free!" they whinge and whine or sulk and complain that they just don't have their illusion any more. How can anyone win with such an absurd attitude? It's impossible. If the smoker doesn't smoke, he feels sad because he cannot have the thing which in reality he himself doesn't want, and if he does smoke, he will be even unhappier as he quickly realises that he is back to where he started.

To successfully navigate the road from child to adult includes accepting that certain things are not real, no matter how wonderful the illusion might be — Father Christmas and the tooth-fairy, for example. Do you remember discovering that Father Christmas/Santa Claus didn't exist? I do very clearly. I was seven years old and it happened in the playground during morning playtime, at Curium infant school, Limassol in Cyprus. It came as a blow and I lived with a certain disappointment for the first couple of days. I then joined in with my parents, keeping the illusion alive for my younger brothers and sisters. (I am the eldest child.) Those of you who are parents or have small children in your lives will understand the immense pleasure that Christmas brings, not so much because of the gifts we adults receive or because we believe in Father Christmas. It is the immense pleasure of making someone else (specifically a child) happy. For parents, that happy and excited look on the faces of the children is a source of immense joy. All of this magic, this joy and fun at Christmas is only possible if we have accepted that Father Christmas is an illusion — a very agreeable one but an illusion nevertheless. There comes a time when we let go of the illusion and live in the reality.

Father Christmas is a wonderful illusion that brings joy and happy memories for the rest of our lives. Even so, we are able to accept and happily live without it. Smoking on the other hand is a disgusting, foul smelling addiction to a drug which does absolutely nothing for you. It just makes you feel bad, anxious and irritable if you can't smoke. I nearly forgot to mention that smokers are condemned to a lifetime of bad breath, less energy, less vitality, the feeling of slavery, the social stigma. What a great illusion! I really want to hang on to that one! So what is there to sacrifice? Absolutely nothing! What is there to 'give up'? Absolutely nothing.

At least with Dumbo, the illusion helped him to do something worthwhile. The smoker just feels bad if he cannot smoke. In his more lucid moments the smoker can see that he gets nothing extra from being a smoker; it does not enable him to fly like a bird or breathe underwater like a fish. After being in one of our sessions, he has it fairly clear that there is no genuine pleasure or benefit; that smoking is utterly pointless, it gives you nothing extra, it just makes you feel like crap if you can't do it.

Look at the people after a great meal. The smokers and non-smokers are, at first glance, both happy. Why? Because it's an enjoyable, happy situation for smokers and non-smokers alike. The difference is that smokers quickly become nervous, panicky and irritable if they cannot smoke. Smokers simply cannot feel as relaxed as non-smokers unless they can smoke. Smoking doesn't make them happier but it sure can destroy whatever potential for pleasure there might be in a situation.

Smokers say smoking is a pleasure. But where is the pleasure? The pleasure is no more than achieving momentary relief from the suffering of being a smoker. Think for a moment, with things that we really enjoy, that give us real pleasure – eating for example, we enjoy them whilst we are doing them. We don't feel anxious, unhappy or stressed if we cannot do them. I love eating ripe mangoes. There is something about the texture of the flesh and the taste which I find unbelievably delicious and even sensual but I certainly don't feel uncomfortable if I don't have mangoes to hand. I've never gone walkabout in my pyjamas looking for mangoes. If you feel anxiety or panic when you can't do something, that means that you don't enjoy it; you suffer from it. It is also one of the clearest indications of drug addiction.

12

Are there no safe substitutes?

I have lost count of the number of times I have heard the comment, "If only smoking wasn't harmful then I wouldn't be here; I'd keep right on smoking." To me that's like saying, "If only gravity and the ground didn't exist, then I would love to throw myself from the 30th floor of my apartment building" and then spending your time complaining how it's not fair that gravity exists. Absurd?!

Such an alternative exists: herbal cigarettes which contain no nicotine, none of the additives that are put into tobacco and are supposedly less carcinogenic. Some manufacturers claim that it is in fact beneficial to smoke some of these herbal cigarettes. (Although I find it difficult to imagine how breathing any sort of smoke into your lungs could be anything but bad for your health.) My experience of herbal cigarettes is that they are very like tobacco. They smell foul, pollute the atmosphere with smoke, make your breath smell, drop ash all over the place, don't do anything for you, cost a fortune and you don't need them. So why isn't everybody smoking these herbal cigarettes? *Because they don't have nicotine in them!* I remember at some time around 1995, a company called Panama Jack (yes, the company that makes the boots) launched nicotine-free cigarettes. The product failed in spite of a massive advertising campaign *because there was no nicotine in them*.

I have also worked with heroin addicts who have said very similar things to me: "If only there was a suitable substitute for heroin." (Methadone doesn't count; it is also highly addictive. All you do is change your pusher.) In these situations, I have proposed that the heroin addict maintain every step of his heroin fix (the ritual of preparation and the social aspect) but that he replaces the heroine in the syringe with saline solution. Do you think that this would work? Obviously not! Why not? *Because the syringe has no heroin in it!*

The irony that many smokers fail to grasp is that the substitute already exists (herbal cigarettes). No one uses them because they provide no 'satisfaction'. Why not? Because it is the addictive drug nicotine that creates the 'dissatisfaction' in the first place and without the constant dissatisfaction, there is nothing to relieve, so smoking herbal cigarettes is quickly seen as it really is: utterly pointless, just a smelly, horrible act of breathing smoke into your lungs.

Quite often a smoker in the session will talk about how he enjoys the taste. Then that same person will tell us in another moment how the awful taste even made him vomit when he started. Frequently I see people who haven't smoked a cigarette in a long time but cannot stop chewing nicotine gum. They tell me the same thing: that at first, the nicotine gum was awful and how they are now completely accustomed to it. The fact is that we will work at and succeed in becoming accustomed to any taste, no matter how awful, so that we can get our nicotine fix.

Even those supposedly 'special' cigarettes which some smokers claim taste the best. Think, what does a smoker do when he runs out of his preferred brand of cigarettes and can only find a brand that he normally wouldn't smoke? Does he stop smoking? No! He'll smoke it anyway. He might pull a face and, whilst lighting another cigarette, say that he doesn't understand how anyone can smoke this 'shit'. But he'll smoke it anyway in spite of the disgusting taste and smell. How can this be? Clearly, he is smoking not for the taste or smell but to get his fix of the drug nicotine.

If anyone truly smoked for the taste, there simply wouldn't be any smokers, as none would have got past smoking that first disgusting cigarette. It is important you understand the following:

The heroin addict gets used to injecting himself with a hypodermic syringe because it relieves the anxiety, panic and emptiness that the drug heroin creates. He will even claim that injecting himself is a 'pleasure'. (If you're not addicted to heroin, you can see very clearly that sticking a needle into your body is not a pleasure.)

The smoker learns to get used to the disgusting taste and smell of a cigarette because it relieves the anxiety, panic and emptiness that nicotine creates. He will even call it his pleasure. (If you're not addicted to nicotine, then you can see very clearly that sticking a cigarette in your mouth and setting fire to it is not a pleasure.)

"Ah!" you say, "The feeling of heroin withdrawal is much stronger than the feeling caused by nicotine withdrawal." I don't dispute that. At least the heroin addict can see that the driving force of his addiction is the withdrawal. He knows with certainty that he needs heroin to relieve the intense heroin withdrawal pangs. In contrast, as smokers, we have suffered light nicotine withdrawal all of our adult lives (ie. we haven't experienced adult life without constant nicotine withdrawal). We confuse the feeling of nicotine withdrawal with normal stress or anxiety or somehow feel that it is an existential emptiness caused simply by being alive, being human. We believe that, although smoking is bad, at least it helps us fill that emptiness. We perceive things as the opposite to what they really are. Smoking does not fill that emptiness. *It is the cause. The empty feeling is nicotine withdrawal.* Accept it! There is nothing to give up or sacrifice.

The tobacco companies are perfectly aware of the fears and desires of smokers (after all they helped create most of them in the first place). They exploited the 'if only there were a safe substitute' mindset with the 'lite' or low-tar versions of each brand. The argument went something like this: why deny yourself the satisfaction of smoking when you can smoke this 'safer – lite' version of your favourite brand which contains less nicotine and less tar than the full-strength version.

The lie underpinning this marketing initiative is that the lite version is somehow 'safer'. It is not safer. If anything, lite cigarettes are more dangerous!

Independent studies showed this and the tobacco industry's own documents show that they knew of this in the '70's and '80's. Most smokers end up inhaling the smoke longer and more deeply. A common experience of our clients who had switched to a lite version of their brand was that they found themselves smoking more. Many smokers reported smoking twice as much which is understandable: if each cigarette contains half the nicotine then logically you will need to smoke twice as much to get the same level of 'satisfaction'.

Smokers talk about the satisfaction of smoking and we have all seen the expression of immense satisfaction on the face of a smoker after taking a massive drag on his cigarette. It has been portrayed so many times in so many different media. As I wrote previously, for something to satisfy there must first necessarily exist a state of dissatisfaction. So what might this be? It's the dissatisfaction caused by the previous cigarette (nicotine withdrawal). And that in a nutshell is why there is no suitable substitute.

The drug creates the need for itself so you cannot get the 'satisfaction' when you take the drug nicotine if you do not suffer the dissatisfaction of nicotine withdrawal between nicotine fixes. In other words, you cannot experience the relief that smoking a cigarette provides (which is relieving nicotine withdrawal), unless you are prepared to systematically poison your body with nicotine.

97

Who would want a substitute for that? You don't need one!

One of the very important instructions in the session is not to use any substitutes. People ask, "Can't I use nicotine patches or gum to help me over the nicotine withdrawal? By putting nicotine into your body, you only succeed in drawing out nicotine withdrawal. However, the withdrawal simply is not the problem. It is the idea that, although it's not good for you, smoking does at least provide some sort of pleasure or help in facing life.

I remember one client in particular, let's call him Javier, who left the session happy to be a non-smoker. He reported back to his doctor asking if he had any advice. The doctor was well-meaning but like most doctors knew next to nothing about how addiction works. His information came mainly from the propaganda created directly and indirectly by the pharmaceutical industry. He recommended (wrongly but not surprisingly) that Javier use nicotine gum or patches to "help with the first few days." Sadly, Javi did just that. His story, as he told it (with humour) went like this:

The nicotine gum tasted awful and after a few days he had a constant bad stomach-ache and his gums had started to bleed (side effects I often hear mentioned by other clients who have used nicotine gum). Because of these side effects, he decided that he would try to wean himself onto normal chewing gum. However, his chewing was so intense that after a couple of weeks or so he felt that his cheek muscles were becoming seriously overdeveloped making him feel increasingly like a hamster. Javi, being a man of many ideas, then thought, "I know… Chupachups!" (Chupachups is a sort of lollipop.) After all, the legend goes that Johann Cruyff (the famous Dutch footballer and trainer) had used them to stop smoking. Javi spent another three weeks sucking like a small child on his lollipop. He said he became utterly sick of the constant sweet, sticky taste in his mouth. Looking around for yet another substitute, he decided on a menthol flavoured plastic cigarette. Javi spent a lot of time during the next few weeks with it stuck in his mouth, until one day whilst out shopping with his wife, he caught sight of himself in a mirror and realised what an utter prat he looked with a plastic cigarette in his mouth. Javi by now had started to feel desperate. He said he felt that he needed yet another substitute to replace the substitute that he'd used to replace the previous substitute etc. As he sat and thought about what to do next, the thought came to him that what might work would be a cigarette. And that is how I came to see him again some three months later.

Why did you start smoking again?

The absurd part of Javi's story is that he had no nicotine in his body when he started chewing the nicotine gum; he was in fact free. If he'd followed my instructions he would have realised that and would have been delighted to be so. Instead, he put nicotine back into his body, then through using different substitutes, managed to keep alive the idea that he needed something. Once he had run out of substitutes he came full circle to the thing which he was trying to substitute in the first place.

One thing that we should all understand is that nicotine is a very powerful and deadly nerve-toxin. Contrary to the way the pharmaceutical industry markets it, it is also a dangerous vasoconstrictor, restricting blood-flow and raising blood-pressure. Just 40mg (a couple of drops) is the lethal dose of nicotine, if injected into a vein. With just this small dose you will discover very quickly if there is an afterlife! (Interestingly, in the film 'Thank you for Smoking', kidnappers almost succeed in murdering a hostage with nicotine patches). It is clear from the marketing and PR that there is competition nowadays to become the preferred supplier of the nicotine addict. I recently saw an advertisement on television, selling nicotine patches. It showed a pretty young girl, riding her scooter. The voiceover didn't talk about freeing the girl of her nicotine addiction; it was simply encouraging the viewer to change 'pusher'. The voiceover wasn't an inspiring, "Free yourself of the slavery of nicotine addiction." It was, *"Take away the smoke but keep the fire."* The message was, "Nicotine is OK, in fact it's exciting and fun and quite daring to use nicotine and if you're intelligent you can get the 'benefits' without the unpleasant effect of the smoke." So what do you think they are trying to do? Free you or get you to change pusher? The commentary says it all! However you look at this, it's pretty scummy. I include here a comment from someone who tried nicotine gum:

I have horrible muscle aches in my body – particularly in my legs. I have been chewing nicotine gum for 6 years now and have unconsciously been chewing more and more. I currently chew 15-20 4mg pieces a day. I am concerned I may be overdosing and causing damage to my muscles. Instead of dying from lung cancer have I doomed myself with irreversible muscle damage? Oh dear, I just didn't want to stink anymore and be able to walk up a flight of stairs without getting out of breath and just be more healthy overall. There are days it hurts just to get out of bed.

The pharmaceutical companies would like to become the preferred supplier to nicotine addicts, whilst the tobacco companies don't want to lose their market share. Let us be absolutely clear that:

- *Nicotine is harmful to every bodily organ.*

99

- *Nicotine has an especially devastating impact on the cardiovascular system.*
- *Nicotine* negatively affects the immune system.

While much marketing attention has been given to the effects of nicotine on the brain, nicotine has harmful effects on every vital organ in the body. In the lungs, nicotine is a primary contributor to lung cancer, emphysema, pneumonia, and chronic bronchitis. Nicotine has been connected to leukaemia and cataracts. It has been strongly associated with cancers of the oesophagus, larynx, throat, mouth, bladder, pancreas, liver, kidneys, cervix, stomach, colon, and rectum. The heart and circulatory systems demonstrate the harmful effects of nicotine through strokes, heart attacks, vascular diseases and aneurysms. In terms of the reproductive system, nicotine increases the risks for infertility and miscarriages in women and impotence and infertility in men. Infants are at risk for low birth weight, premature delivery and lung problems when their mothers use nicotine during their pregnancies. The immune system is affected and individuals addicted to nicotine seem to be more prone to infectious illnesses such as colds and the flu. (See Ref. 5.)

So why on earth would you want to put nicotine into your body for any reason at all? Especially as studies show that your chances of stopping with NRT (in reality Cigarette Replacement Therapy) and *cojones* are less than if you stop with *cojones* alone. (Ref. 1)

Would you seriously ever think of helping an alcoholic free himself by supplying him with beer instead of whisky? Of course not! You'd have to be an utter moron to fall for that one! Or would you? Well, unfortunately that is exactly what has happened in western society. Smokers, the population in general including the medical profession have been manipulated into believing something that goes against all logic, common sense and independent evidence, but is mind-bogglingly profitable for the pharmaceutical industry.

Remember, a smoker stops smoking because he hates being a smoker. He's sick and tired of feeling sick and tired. Cutting down doesn't work. If it did, he would be smoking just those few and would feel no need to stop. There is no such thing as the occasional or special cigarette, just the life of a nicotine addict – a smoker. Think just for a moment: to spend your life feeling unhappy or sad because you cannot have something that you yourself don't want. That is beyond absurd.

There truly is nothing to give up and nothing to sacrifice. You don't need a substitute. The cigarette does absolutely nothing for you. All you have ever been trying to do is get back to feeling as relaxed and as comfortable as you did before you started smoking and the only thing stopping you… you guessed it… *is the next cigarette*. Why on earth would you need a substitute for that? What would be the point?

This mental manipulation is compounded by the information put out by 'experts'. Practically all of the organisations upon which we depend for help have been seriously compromised by the pharmaceutical industry's propaganda and money and have become little more than mouth-pieces for the industry. We consult our GPs, most of whom have had little or no training on addiction and depend either directly or indirectly on the information (pseudo-science/marketing) put out by the pharmaceutical companies.

Doctors are experts in the consequences of smoking. They are not experts in freeing people of their addictions. The simple truth is that most medical advice about how to stop smoking is wrong. Scare campaigns don't work. The pharmaceutical industry distorts both medical and public perception of the problem through questionable 'scientific' studies (which are in fact no more than marketing), bribing doctors and decision makers. They make lucrative alliances with the 'experts', the NGO's and the government. *The pharmaceutical industry has no effective response to nicotine addiction* but manages to sell literally thousands of millions of euros worth of pointless treatments. In Spain, societies such as SEDET (Spanish Society of Experts in 'Tabaquismo') have been set up with, it would appear, the objective of creating an official club to support the pharmaceutical companies' agenda. The net result of these cosy and questionable relationships between the pharmaceutical industry, the 'experts', trusted associations, health companies and the government *is that smokers are always the losers.* They are advised to use techniques and medication to stop smoking which in many cases actually reduce their chances of success and can, in the case of drugs such as Zyban and Champix, produce horrific side effects – even death, all in the name of profit. (See references 1, 2 and 7 at end of the book.) Inevitably after much suffering, most smokers fail to stop and are left with the impression that it is they and not the techniques, gimmicks, drugs or worthless advice that are at fault. The result of this is the enrichment of the few at the cost of the suffering of many.

Geoffrey Molloy

13

I only need the doctor to say something to stop smoking

This comment is common particularly amongst younger smokers. They realise that they are addicted but they still feel young and strong. They do not relate their own situation to the suffering experienced by the smoker dying of lung cancer, emphysema or any other of the slow painful deaths caused by smoking. The smoker thinks about stopping smoking, thinks it would be nice not to do it but there is no rush to stop and will say something like, "Well, I only need the doctor to say something to stop smoking." By this I don't mean the generalised warnings that all doctors give to all smoking patients. The hope is that somehow the doctor will detect the early signs and symptoms of something going wrong (ie. a smoking related disease) and warn you before it becomes too serious. You hope that when this moment arrives, the advice of the doctor will be sufficient motivation to stop smoking.

What on earth makes you believe that? What do you think all of those five million smokers who died last year of a horrible smoking related disease thought? There are some smokers who, on receiving news that they already have lung cancer, stop smoking but of course it's too late. Over the years I have treated thousands of people but the most poignant moments have been those moments shared with clients who are already sick.

So let's look at the whole idea of fear as a technique for stopping smoking, especially the fear of illness. Governments and their 'experts' resort principally to fear and pharmaceuticals as a way of stopping smoking. These are the least effective tools.

Stopping smoking is not difficult. Smokers do it every day, usually because of the horrible effects of smoking. How many times have you said or thought at the end of the day, "Right this time I'm serious; tomorrow I will definitely stop smoking"? We normally make the decision at the end of the day when we are feeling sick and saturated with the 4,000 odd chemical compounds found in tobacco smoke. But this is no different to overeating. If you have overeaten, then the mere sight of

103

food, even if it's your favourite dish, will provoke nausea. The feeling however soon passes and before long the question pops into your head, "So what's for dinner then?"

In exactly the same way, when you are saturated with all the toxic chemicals in a cigarette, your head aches and your chest hurts; then just like the overstuffed diner, the idea of more makes you feel queasy. However, once the symptoms of poisoning subside, the thought comes into your head, "I fancy a cigarette."

A similar thing happens with the fear sell. I had a client, a doctor, a forensic pathologist in fact, who smoked some two to three packs a day. He was desperate to free himself of his nicotine addiction and had made many failed attempts to stop, most of which lasted only a few hours. He explained to me that he had once stopped smoking for three weeks after they removed a tumour from his lungs! A tumour in his lungs which he explained in all probability was related to his smoking, provided sufficient motivation for just three weeks. Being a forensic pathologist meant that he was fully aware of just how dangerous smoking was for him in particular. He also explained that he felt incredibly stupid for smoking but simply felt unable to stop. Did fear help this man stop? Absolutely not! It increased his desire to stop but at the same time made it even more difficult to do so. He did finally stop after many sessions and many hours of work.

On another occasion I was about to begin a session in Barcelona when a client arrived, accompanied by a helper pushing a low trolley upon which was a large, white machine about the size of a three-door filing cabinet, lying on its back. The machine had several warnings stuck on the outside: 'Oxygen no naked flame'. A lady was connected to this machine by a clear plastic hose which lead to her nostrils. The woman walked very slowly to her seat, sat down, removed the tubes from her nose and lit a cigarette. The alarm on the faces of the other clients was quite apparent. A well-dressed man of about forty became quite agitated. He addressed himself to me, "Well, this is very American, I suppose that you've arranged this to frighten us, right?" I explained that I myself felt both shocked and nervous mainly because, in spite of the warnings on the machine, the woman was smoking right next to it. During the session the woman explained to us that she suffered from emphysema and that her lung capacity was reduced to 15%. She still smoked two packs a day. The lady died without ever managing to stop smoking. Trying to stop smoking once you have a terminal disease is rather like trying to solve a maths problem whilst being suspended by your ankles from the window of a 30th floor apartment. The question is, is it easier to solve the problem in a normal setting or dangling terrified, upside down, a hundred metres in the air?

Fear does not work as a way of stopping smoking. Stopping smoking for the reasons you shouldn't smoke does not work in the long term. You might be able to stop whilst the fear is fresh in your mind and acts as a brake to your desire or perceived need, but once the fear response ends, you are left once again with your desire to smoke and no brake. Think, one of the moments in which a smoker lights a cigarette is when he feels anxious. So tell a smoker that he has a killer disease related to smoking and what is his most likely reaction? Why, light a cigarette of course. In many cases fear leads directly to increased consumption. Imagine that you're drinking your coffee and reading your newspaper. You turn the page and suddenly you are confronted with a full-page report on smoking, the diseases and dangers together with photographs of the same. What is your reaction? I have asked this question of many smokers and most say, "Immediately turn the page" and about half say, "Turn the page and light a cigarette." They say that they know their reaction is stupid but they cannot help it; the situation stresses them and they feel the need to smoke.

Many governments have obliged cigarette manufacturers to place large, written and graphic warnings on cigarette packs. These warnings are nowadays largely invisible to the average smoker. Perhaps the biggest impact of these warnings in Spain was to increase the sales of cigarette pouches which many smokers purchased to hide the warnings. The sudden increase in the number of clients with pouches was noticeable in our sessions. However, nowadays hardly anyone uses them. Smokers have learnt to 'tune out' the warnings. The warnings also give youngsters a chance for bravado and humour. A few years ago I was standing in line at a petrol station waiting to pay. A young man in front of me asked for a packet of Marlboro. The girl duly gave him the pack. The first thing he did was to study the warning which said 'Smoking causes Impotence'. He said out aloud, "Fuck me! Impotence! Can you change the pack please? I prefer the cancer ones." Really effective what? A recent study showed that these labels do not reduce smoking and can even increase consumption. (See Reference 8.)

The vast majority (more than 95%) of smokers who have a fatal or debilitating smoking related disease have already been told by their doctor before and during their illness that they must stop smoking. They have been exposed to the government messages that smoking is dangerous for years. None of them wanted their disease. None of them wanted to end up like that. But there they are.

Geoffrey Molloy

14

The use of drugs and NRT (Cigarette Replacement Therapy) to stop smoking

Nicotine withdrawal exists. Some people are aware of certain sensations whilst the body eliminates nicotine. These symptoms are very light, so light in fact that they don't even wake you up when you're asleep. These symptoms are usually called 'nicotine withdrawal'. Unfortunately, many people confuse the hysterics ("I want to smoke but cannot") with physical withdrawal.

Nicotine has a half-life of about 90 minutes. This means that in 90 minutes your body will have eliminated 50% of the nicotine introduced. Nicotine withdrawal is very light. It is so light as to be almost unnoticeable. I have often wished that the nicotine withdrawal were a bit stronger, as it would help smokers see the nature of the nicotine scam more clearly. There would also be fewer smokers.

The tobacco industry exploited this fact (the barely perceptible withdrawal) for many years, claiming that smoking was not an addiction, just a habit. The fact is that smokers suffer nicotine withdrawal continuously. That, together with the constant mental manipulation, is what keeps them smoking. Nicotine withdrawal symptoms are often described as consisting of bad temper, irritability, difficulty in concentrating, anxiety and so on. No differentiation is made between the psychological and physical aspects. Our experience is that 98% of what normally is recognized as nicotine withdrawal in the mind and 2% is physical.

I have heard literally hundreds of people complain about their nicotine withdrawal: bad temper, inability to concentrate, anxiety, feeling down. They are convinced that the cause of all of this suffering is physical nicotine withdrawal. Many fear having to pass through the same suffering yet again. However, many of these very same smokers who complained of the severity of the withdrawal in previous attempts, comment that when they stopped smoking in one of our sessions, the withdrawal was barely noticeable and even pleasurable. That was also my experience. Once I understood what was happening and stopped feeling that I was somehow being deprived, then the physical withdrawal all but disappeared. I was aware of the physical withdrawal but it caused no suffering. I felt a sense of relief that I was eliminating the drug nicotine from my body for good.

Why then is so much utter nonsense spoken about the physical withdrawal symptoms? It is because the main nicotine vendors (Big Tobacco and Big Pharma) want it that way. Otherwise, how are they going to sell their product or keep you hooked? And the people and organisations that we depend on to defend us, do not. Lately, these two industries have made great efforts to present nicotine as being 'all right/not so bad'. Some industry funded academics have even tried to equate nicotine addiction to taking caffeine in coffee. This is such an outrageous, bare-faced lie. The fatal dose for nicotine is 40-60 mg. for a 70 kilo person whilst the fatal dose of caffeine would be 10,000 mg. I remind you once again of the 'Golden Rule':

'He who has the gold makes the rules.'

This rule may be seen operating at all levels of our society. This golden rule is responsible, in a large part, for the disease, suffering and general lack of wellbeing in our society. Big Pharma and Big Tobacco have managed to subvert trusted, supposedly independent associations and NGO's by 'donating' large sums of money, by lobbying (which again involves the distribution of gifts and money) at government and institutional level.

The use of these drugs and substitutes to stop smoking is a lucrative scam perpetrated by Big Pharma on the general public. Big Pharma has, through use of its immense financial power, distorted public and medical opinion to enhance perception of the product's (drug's) effectiveness whilst playing down the horrible (sometimes fatal) side effects. There are two basic categories of therapy:

The incorrectly named Nicotine Replacement Therapy (NRT). It should be called '*Cigarette* Replacement Therapy'. Why? Because you stop smoking but carry on taking the very drug which causes the addiction in the first place. You replace nicotine with nicotine. The smoker remains addicted to nicotine; he just obtains it in a different format. Various studies have shown that many smokers have become addicted to the replacement nicotine source. This is borne out by experience at our sessions.

Practically every *independent* and *well-designed study, or meta-analysis of the data* of NRT (CRT) has shown it to be ineffective or even reducing the chances of success. (See Reference 1. again.)

Why did you start smoking again?

Nicotine withdrawal would have no effect whatsoever if it were not for the erroneous mental map that tells us we cannot face life without a cigarette; that by stopping we have to sacrifice something. It is in fact this sense of sacrifice which is at the root of all difficulties when a person tries to stop smoking (or any drug for that matter) and is caused by the way we perceive the drug – in other words by our beliefs, our mental model.

You cannot change a person's beliefs or modify his mental model using more of the same drug or by giving them a pill.

The other Big Pharma stop-smoking offering are pills that alter brain chemistry. Now I don't know about you but I would not want, under any circumstances, that corporations with the track record of the big pharmaceutical companies, give me chemicals that alter my brain-chemistry and thus my mental functioning, especially when you take into account that they are not necessary, nor even very effective. Let's get this into perspective.

For a moment, imagine that you have a very serious disease. You know that there is a 50% chance that it will kill you and if it doesn't kill you, you know that it will gradually destroy your quality of life. You will feel gradually more and more tired; it will make you smell bad, discolour your teeth, ruin your skin whilst taking away your confidence. You seek a cure from your doctor. He says that there are two available:

The first will alter your brain chemistry and might produce horrific side effects, up to and including death. The drug is expensive and in spite of these side effects, not very effective. In fact, based on negative incident reports, the relevant authorities I many countries (including the FDA in the USA) have issued the strongest possible warnings about the dangers associated with these drugs. Added to this is the fact that the drug does not treat the cause of the illness, only the symptoms.

Now we come to the second possibility, a treatment which does not require any pharmaceuticals or other chemicals. It is far more effective and has no side effects.

Which would you choose? You don't even need a brain to answer that question

Some years ago we were featured in a program about stopping smoking made by Tele5 in Spain. In this program the company doctor from AT&T who had implemented our program successfully, was asked by the reporter why he had chosen our program over other methods of stopping smoking (ie. pharmaceutical). His response was interesting. He stated that he had already tried the pharmaceutical solutions and that our programme was, in his experience, the most effective. But what he particularly liked was that there were no possible side effects. He explained that as a doctor, his mission was not only to cure people but to avoid doing harm. He felt that he could not morally justify exposing his patients to unnecessary danger when such an innocuous, safe and effective alternative existed.

The problem is that most doctors either don't have or make the time to investigate the effectiveness of their treatments. They tend to accept the studies and publicity produced by Big Pharma. Remember the hammer and nail syndrome: 'If the only tool you've got is a hammer, then all problems will look like nails'. If your principle tool is pharmaceutical, then when confronted with addiction, it is likely that your question will be, "Which pharmaceutical can I use to solve this problem?"

The AT&T doctor was able to think independently and step outside of the hammer and nail syndrome. He also had a very genuine interest in the welfare of his patients.

In our sessions I have heard of many bad experiences of people taking these pharmaceuticals. Some nearly lost their lives; others simply felt so sick that they stopped the treatment. (I urge you to look at references 2 and 7 for a list of the side effects of these drugs.) A teacher told me how Chantix caused her confusion and anxiety so that she would forget what she had been talking about just a moment earlier. This happened to her on various occasions whilst she was teaching. You can imagine how distressing this must have been for her. For me the most sinister aspect of her experience was that when she complained of these side effects to her doctor he insisted that the effects she felt were not related to Chantix, even though similar side effects were described in the literature provided by the manufacturer and the symptoms stopped as soon as she stopped taking the drug.

Just to finish this chapter, I am always very happy to learn that someone has stopped smoking, irrespective of the method they used. Freeing oneself from an addiction is immensely satisfying and one of the most positive steps that anyone can take in life. It is one of the very few decisions that you know from the moment you take it and for the rest of your life, that the decision was the correct one.

Many people in our sessions have paid a lot of money for these pharmacological treatments and have suffered anything from mildly uncomfortable to life-threatening side effects. Why run this unnecessary risk when, just by reading a book or speaking with a therapist, you can not only stop smoking but feel happy about it as well? The problem with nicotine addiction is the same as with any addiction. It is not so much the physical withdrawal symptoms; it is the way in which we perceive the

Why did you start smoking again?

drug that causes the problem. In other words, we need to change our mental model — something that we cannot change with a pill.

Geoffrey Molloy

15

My problem is that I have an addictive personality; it's genetic...

...which means that I cannot stop smoking and am doomed to smoke the whole of my life.

Here we have a real 'cracker'. So much utter crap is spoken about addictive personalities when in reality, the idea is no more than a notion. The idea has absolutely no scientific basis. Let's take a closer look at this.

Whilst I was addicted to nicotine, my behaviour was that of a drug addict. During that time I could say that I had an addictive personality. I indulged in self destructive behaviour. I did something which I knew rationally was damaging me but felt I simply couldn't live without it. I was less vital, more stressed and constantly anxious to ensure that I always had a more than adequate supply of my drug.

But my personality didn't cause my addiction. Nicotine and the comprehensive manipulation of my mental maps caused my addiction, just as it did for more than 80% of adults in the sixties and seventies. For many it continues to do so today. What my addiction did do was modify my behaviour.

Addicts do not have addictive personalities but they do have addictive behaviour.

If anyone who stops using nicotine or any other drug for that matter, feels that they have made a sacrifice, then it is likely that they will search for some sort of substitute. This does not mean that they have addictive personalities. The 'I've got an addictive personality' argument is simply another way of saying, "I smoke but I don't know why." It is also a very convenient excuse; "It's not my fault I smoke, it's my personality, something in my upbringing." However, even better is the argument, "I cannot stop smoking; it's genetic."

The self-appointed experts' view on drug addiction is often based on something known as 'The Twelve Step Programme'. The best known of these programmes is AA (Alcoholics Anonymous). There is also NA

(Narcotics Anonymous), OA (Overeaters Anonymous), SA (Smokers Anonymous) and so it goes on. The theory put forward by these people and others who should know better (and would do if they just stopped to check out the evidence with an open mind), is that we are born as drug addicts and that there is nothing we can do about it, apart from accept that we are not 'normal'. Our genes mean that we are doomed. This idea has distorted so many lives, caused so much misery and inhibited the personal growth of so many people.

Take obesity for example. There is lot of rubbish talked about obesity being caused by 'fatty' genes (mostly asserted by fat people and the 'everything-depends-on-your-genes' brigade.) Listen really carefully. Fatness in 99% of cases is caused by eating too much of the wrong food and lack of exercise. If 'fatty' genes and therefore 'thinny' genes existed, then one would expect that the ratio of fat people to thin people would be more or less steady, both historically and geographically. "Ah," you say, "Fat parents often have fat kids." This is not usually because of their genes but because they tend to have the same eating habits as their parents. Children tend to have similar tastes to their parents. Parents got fat eating in a certain way; kids get fat eating in the same way. My father died at age 53, weighing close on to 150 kilos. I am 5cm taller than him and weigh some 55 kilos less. However, if I drank and ate as he did, I have no doubt whatsoever that my weight would be similar. I eat much less than he did; I eat much healthier than he did and I do not drink vast quantities of alcohol as he did; I do more exercise, therefore I am not as fat. I have been fatter and thinner at different times in my life and have found the determining factors to be the amount and type of food I eat, together with the amount of physical exercise I do.

We all believe that we live in the most advanced and scientific human society that has ever existed. But western society has believed that of itself more or less since the Renaissance. The Chinese believed that of their society more than 3,000 years ago. The Arabs believed that of their society some 600 years ago. We uncritically swallow much of the oversimplified and misleading scientific information available. It is fashionable nowadays to think that everything depends on your genes.

Most people have an oversimplified idea of the significance of genes and how they act. Every so often some clown touts the simplistic, sensational headline *'Gene for alcoholism found', 'Gene for obesity found'*. **There are no such genes.** Often, this is no more than thinly disguised marketing by the health industry. The marketing message goes like this: If you have a genetic problem that causes some sort of chemical imbalance, then obviously you will need some sort of pill (hopefully expensive) or surgical procedure (also expensive but available on finance) to correct it. Because if it's genetic that means the machine (your body) doesn't work properly and does not have the ability to correct the imbalance or fault which conveniently requires expensive pills or surgery.

Smokers smoke because it's genetic? Let's check out some facts: In Spain, like in many other countries, just thirty years ago some 80% of the adult population smoked. Nowadays, the figure is closer to 30%. So what are we to believe? If we use the 'everything-depends-on-your-genes' argument, we are forced to conclude that during the past thirty years a massive, spontaneous, genetic mutation has occurred within the population? Whilst this is possible, it is highly improbable. But if you are convinced that everything depends on genes, then you will believe that it must be so.

Quite a few years ago a client freed himself of his nicotine and alcohol addictions in my sessions. Let's call him Pedro (not his real name). He was delighted. I know this because several months later he dropped me a line to let me know just how happy he was; that he no longer needed either alcohol or nicotine. He told me that he didn't miss them and that his only regret was that he had not discovered us sooner. I was very pleased for him. His whole attitude and demeanour had changed for the better. Some weeks later I received a call from his brother, a psychologist who asked why I had told Pedro that he was free. I replied, "Look at him, he's happy, doesn't feel that he needs these drugs; he doesn't miss them and is delighted to be free; on top of that it is clear that he feels that he is growing as a person." At this reply the man became irritated, saying that his brother Pedro could never be free, that he was an addict born that way and that for him there was no cure. I asked, "If Pedro was born an alcoholic, then could he be an alcoholic without ever having drunk alcohol?" He replied, "Yes". How do you get around such unthinking, ingrained stupidity from someone who is a 'professional' in their field?

"Ah," you say, "but everyone knows that 'once a smoker always a smoker'. If an ex-smoker takes just one puff he will become addicted again." This has nothing to do with his personality, but the nature of drug addiction. An ex-smoker can never smoke 'just one cigarette'.

Get this clear. The idea of smoking one cigarette is an illusion; it always was and what's more, it always will be. *You the smoker never could smoke just one cigarette; that's why you're reading this.* Just like the millions of youngsters who thought that they'd just try one, you too got hooked and found yourself a victim of the nicotine scam. You never decided to become a smoker; you decided just to experiment with one cigarette. Here you are, many years and hundreds of thousands of cigarettes later. Each one of the cigarettes that you have smoked was the direct result of the illusion 'just one cigarette' – something that simply doesn't exist

The reason that an ex-smoker cannot smoke just one cigarette is that she never could. It has nothing to do with personality or genes. It has to do with the nature of the addictive drug nicotine and the wrong (manipulated) mental map. If you go for a while without smoking and then you light a cigarette (for whatever reason), you will get hooked again, usually much faster than when you first started. Why? Because you don't need to learn how to smoke again. The reason is that you have already learnt to smoke and once you learn something you cannot unlearn it.

Let's compare this with learning how to ride a bike. Usually we learn as small children. The key aspect of riding a bike is to find your balance. Once you have mastered that aspect, even if you don't ride a bike for one, five or even ten years, you know that you will never forget. Ask this question of anyone. They will be confident that, irrespective of the number of years they have passed without riding a bike, they need no time at all to learn again. The same could be said of driving a car, playing chess, swimming, riding a horse or controlling your bladder, You will never unlearn what you have learnt. Jolly good thing too in my view. However, we don't ever feel depressed about this. I've yet to hear anyone complain, "Once a cyclist, always a cyclist! I know I'll never be free of bicycles." We simply accept that we cannot unlearn something we've learnt; in fact we correctly see it as an advantage. Imagine if you had to learn to drive every time you got into your car or to learn to swim each time you went to the swimming-pool, life would be very different.

Responsibility: The 'addictive personality, it's my genes' argument is the perfect excuse to avoid responsibility. "I smoke and cannot stop but there is nothing I can do about it; you see, it's genetic; I've got nicotine addict genes; I simply can't do anything about my genes." Well, that gets the smoker off the hook with family and friends. "Don't give me a hard time for being a smoker. I know it's stupid and dangerous but there is nothing I can do about it; it's genetic." Big Tobacco and Big Pharma are happy with this state of affairs. Why? Simply because, if you believe it's genetic, this belief will undermine your resolve and make it less likely that you will succeed at stopping smoking. Whilst smokers believe this manipulated mental model, they will resort to pharmaceuticals and substitutes for a solution. The logic goes like this: "If my disease/addiction is genetic, that means that I am somehow flawed or imperfect and I clearly do not have within me that which I need to free myself. I must look outside to correct this situation; I will have to resort to pharmaceuticals, surgery or magic."

You are enough. You don't need anything else, especially not an addictive, dangerous, expensive drug such as nicotine which leaves you less vital, smelling worse, with stained teeth, bad breath and feeling constantly more stressed than if you didn't smoke. Some smokers have told me, "I don't feel like me if I don't smoke." If you have smoked all of your adult life, you will only ever have felt 'complete' whilst smoking a cigarette. Even then, you will often have felt that one cigarette wasn't enough. Remember, it is the nicotine that makes you feel incomplete in the first place. My own experience is a good example of the powerful way in which the mental maps determine how you understand your experience.

I tried for many years and on many occasions to stop smoking. I couldn't do it. I would feel so stressed and bad tempered that I would always start again. Two people close to me died as a result of smoking: one from heart attack and the other of lung cancer. I hoped that these events would scare me and provide me with sufficient motivation to stop smoking. They didn't; if anything they made me more anxious and I smoked more. I tried many different ways to stop smoking: patches, gum, aversion therapy, herbal remedies, amongst others. I read about and believed the convincing sounding arguments for addictive personalities. I read also the scientific sounding but largely irrelevant nonsense about receptors in our neurons and how genes could modify the chemical environment in the brain. Added to this, my father was an alcoholic so I had (at least superficially) strong evidence that it was probably genetic.

I was convinced that I had either some genetic flaw that made me a nicotine addict or had an addictive personality or probably both. I truly felt hopeless. Many nights I would say something like, "Right that's it, this is my last cigarette! Tomorrow I will stop smoking." Inevitably, the next morning it would seem too difficult. As I lit my first cigarette I would despise myself for not being able to stop, whilst feeling helpless to do anything about it.

Something sinister started to happen; I occasionally suffered a pain in my calf muscles during the night. These pains were severe enough to wake me up. I suspected it might be Buerger's disease. Buerger's disease involves the loss of circulation to the extremities and is directly related to tobacco use, both smoked and chewed. It results in ulcers, necrosis and gangrene and often culminates in amputation. The process is progressive. If the smoker does not stop smoking he will usually suffer a progressive series of amputations which often leaves the person without legs or fingers. I didn't dare go to the doctor, just in case it was something horrible, such as Buerger's disease. I knew that stopping smoking stops the disease but I believed that I couldn't stop smoking. I would wake up at three or four in the morning with pain in my calf muscles, quietly get out of bed so as not to disturb my wife and walk in darkness into the lounge where I would smoke several cigarettes. Those were dark moments indeed. I felt depressed, convinced that I was doing something that would kill me, but felt unable to stop.

A book came to my hands. The author was an American psychologist (female) whose name I cannot remember. Her book will have done untold damage to those smokers unfortunate enough to have read it, in a desire to understand the nature of their addiction and to free themselves. In her book she talked specifically about how people who carry on smoking in spite of the symptoms of a disease, do so because they are self-destructive individuals who probably have a hidden death or self-destruct wish. I came to suspect she was probably right as I simply couldn't find an explanation to why I kept on smoking. I came to believe that I did have an addictive personality and that it probably had some genetic component. The nights that I woke up without pain in my legs, I also smoked. I can remember thinking, "I'm such an addict that I even wake up at nights to smoke." I became resigned to my fate as a hopeless case. It was depressing.

In 1993 I stopped smoking. Since that time I have not felt that I have an addictive personality or a secret death-wish. I still sometimes wake up during the night but I know it is not related to smoking. I was a heavy smoker and now I am free. My behaviour has changed but not my personality. I realise that the sense of depression, the sense of hopelessness had nothing to do with an addictive personality. It was caused by my addiction to nicotine. I didn't have an addictive personality but I did have addictive *behaviour*. I didn't stop smoking due to a mutation of my genes (from smoker's genes to non-smoker's genes). What radically changed was my perception of smoking and the drug nicotine. I stopped seeing smoking as I had been manipulated to see it. Instead, I saw it as it really is. Once that happened, my desire to smoke evaporated and I was free. We offer stop-smoking sessions to all smokers, together with a genuine money-back guarantee, irrespective of their genes.

16

But smoking helps me control my weight!
...I would love to be a non-smoker but a slim non-smoker

This is one of the most frequently mentioned worries (and most frequently used excuses) of smokers thinking about stopping smoking. The typical comment is, "I want to be a non-smoker but not a fat non-smoker." Of course 'everyone knows' that it's pretty well obligatory to get fat when you stop smoking. It may even be permanent. Women are particularly worried about this, especially after Easter when they (and some men) start thinking about summer on the beach and 'Operation Bikini'.

The idea that smoking is an effective way of controlling your weight is a myth. If smoking were effective as a method of weight control, then it would be unusual to see a fat smoker. You only have to look around you outside any bar or cafeteria to see that this is not the case. I did just that this morning in the bar where I habitually take my morning coffee. From the youngsters in their twenties to the older guys in their sixties, eleven of the fourteen smokers huddled around the beer barrels used now as a place to put your ashtray, fags and coffee, were overweight! Look around you. How many of the smokers that you know are at their correct weight? Some are; many are not. What is abundantly clear is that there are many fat smokers.

I recently read in the newspapers that smoking helps reduce your weight because it stimulates the expression of a gene which helps keep you slim. Any newspaper that printed a story that held out hope to its readers that nicotine is a slimming aid were indulging in sensationalist nonsense. They clearly did not bother to investigate the story. The study was in fact *a laboratory test carried out on mice*. The connection is at best tenuous and the proof is a long way from being conclusive.

The study does not at any time claim that smoking makes you thin.

But think for just a moment. Does it make sense to control your weight with a toxic and addictive drug which progressively reduces the quality of life of all its users and goes on to horrifically kill half of them? Apart from killing more than five million people a year, it also gives you stained teeth, bad breath, poor skin and less energy. You don't even need a brain to come to the conclusion that using nicotine is a ridiculous strategy to control your weight. However, for a moment, let us assume that you the reader has only half a brain (hypothetically and no offence meant) and so you think absurdly that yes, using such a drug is a good idea, I have a suggestion for you. How about using another addictive drug such as heroin? I have seen a lot of fat smokers but I have yet to see a fat heroin addict, so why not use heroin instead? What would you think if a heroin addict justified his addiction by saying that he knows that heroin is very bad and that he would like to stop using it, but at least it helps him control his weight? Stupid, right? The use of nicotine to control weight is equally absurd. (I am using heroin here as an example and what I have written is in no way meant to condone the use of heroin in any way, shape or form.)

Think, non-smokers also have weight problems and many manage to face and overcome these problems without resorting to addictive, toxic drugs.

So let's have a look at the physiological changes that might impact your weight when you stop smoking. By understanding these changes we can avoid the weight trap.

Over millions of years of evolution your body (which can be thought of as a chemical factory) has evolved a control system known as homeostasis. Homeostasis is a chemical feedback and control system that has evolved to maintain the internal environment of your body within the best parameters for correct functioning. For example: the correct pH, the correct blood-sugar level, the correct temperature, the correct hydration, the correct oxygen levels. Thanks to this marvellous system, your body is capable of adapting to many changes in the environment. When you put into your body a nerve toxin such as nicotine (together with the thousands of other toxic chemicals in a cigarette), your body adapts to protect itself in order to maintain correct functioning. Once you stop smoking your body needs time to eliminate the toxins, adjust and return to correct functioning (its natural healthy state). Trust your body; it knows what it needs to do.

The changes of interest to us are the following:

Metabolic: Nicotine increases your heart rate and through a chemical reaction, makes more sugar available in your blood stream. The response of your homeostatic mechanism (to maintain your body within the correct limits) is to reduce the corresponding work done by your body in this area. Once you stop smoking, your body immediately starts the process of nicotine elimination and is left without the additional sugar-liberating effect previously produced by the nicotine. Your body needs time to increase its sugar-liberating activities. During this period (normally about three weeks or so), you may experience a desire for sweet things (this is your body trying to boost sugar levels). The ex-smoker now starts to eat sweet things (chocolate for example).

If you use food to elevate blood-sugar levels, it takes up to 20 minutes from the time you chew and swallow the food before it is released to the blood. Nicotine, by working through a drug interaction causes the body to release its own stores of sugar, not in 20 minutes but usually in a matter of seconds. In a sense, your body has not had to release sugar on its own in years; you have done it by using nicotine's drug effect!

This is one of the reasons many people gorge themselves on food when they stop smoking. The recently arrived non-smoker experiences a drop in blood-sugar and instinctively reaches for something sweet. You finish your snack, but don't feel completely satisfied. *Remember that although it only takes a minute or two to eat, your blood-sugar isn't boosted for another 18 minutes.* Since you do not feel immediately better, the temptation is to continue eating more and more food, minute by minute until you finally do start to feel better. Watch out! You can eat a lot of food in 20 minutes. This can be repeated numerous times throughout the day. You quickly become accustomed to this level of consumption. (the more you eat the more you want to eat). The equation is simple. You've increased your calorie intake whilst keeping your activity at the same level. The result of this is precisely what you would expect from anyone who starts to eat more whilst keeping their activity levels the same; you get fatter. We'll come back to this in a moment.

Solution: The surest way of avoiding this trap is to make sure that you have fresh fruit to hand during the first days − soft fruit such as grapes, plums, tangerines, oranges, melon. If that is not possible, then fruit juice will do. Note that the fresher the fruit, the better it is, as there are many more vitamins, minerals and other nutrients in fresh fruit as opposed to manipulated or processed food. (If it is not a piece of fruit just as it came off the vine or tree, then it is manipulated or processed.) If you feel you need to eat something sweet, eat fruit or drink a fruit juice and then wait 25 minutes to see how you feel. You will find that the sugar in the fruit is quickly absorbed by your body and will put an end to the feeling that you need to eat something sweet. Also remember the twenty minute rule when you sit down to eat.

Get up from the table feeling that you could still manage to eat a little more.

Peristalsis: Peristalsis is the name given to describe the rhythmic muscular contractions of the intestine which move the food between the stomach and anus. Nicotine provokes an increase in this peristaltic activity. (Many smokers take advantage of this effect by starting their day sitting on the loo and smoking a cigarette which has the effect of stimulating a bowel movement.) Once you stop smoking, the level of peristaltic activity drops until the body adjusts. For some, this can mean a short-lived and not very serious constipation which can make you feel bloated and uncomfortable and give rise to short term weight-gain.

Solution: To avoid problems in this department it's best to eat – yes, you guessed it – fruit. I recommend at least a couple of kiwis or some prunes first thing in the morning and at some time during the day (better before meals rather than after).

Absorption: Nicotine increases production of mucus within the lining of the large intestine. This impedes the efficient absorption of nutrients. The smoker cannot therefore take full advantage of the nutrients in his food. Soon after stopping smoking, the smoker's intestinal mucus returns to normal and the smoker can and thus gets more nutritional value out of the same food. Those people prone to do so, might complain, "That means I cannot eat so much," as if recovering correct body functioning were some sort of sacrifice. Imagine that I come to your house and fix your heating boiler to work more efficiently, after which you find that you need much less fuel to get the same effect. Would you complain about that? Of course not.

Solution: Remember that you are going through a period of adjustment, not because you have stopped smoking but because you started. You have spent many years with your body in a pathological state and you have grown used to this. Once you have stopped smoking, you need to give yourself time to discover and enjoy what works for you. If you follow the 25 minute rule and always leave the table feeling as if you could eat a little more, then you shouldn't have any problem.

Water Retention: Once you stop smoking your body will begin a process of elimination. As the toxins come out of your tissues they will be eliminated, amongst other routes, through urine, perspiration and mucus. However, as these toxins come out of your tissues, the level of acidity may increase and your body may retain water in order to neutralise it. This sometimes creates a sort of bloating effect which happens rapidly, stays for a few days and then disappears. Many women are used to this feeling of retention as they experience it just before they menstruate.

Solution: If you find yourself bloating because of water retention you can accept it as part of the process or you can take a mild, natural diuretic such as horsetail, making sure that you follow the instructions closely. You can reduce water retention by helping your body eliminate all those poisons faster. This you can do by drinking more water, eating fruit on an empty stomach, ideally at breakfast. (Pineapple and melon are especially effective.) Rebounding and swimming are great exercises to speed up the process.

Substitutes and rewards: A common cause of weight gain after stopping smoking is the idea that after you stop smoking, you will need some sort of substitute or reward. The fact is that you don't need either. Nicotine addiction is a pointless nightmare. You don't need a substitute or reward once you have freed yourself of a disease, right? Imagine freeing yourself of a case of genital herpes and saying to yourself, "I no longer have genital herpes, what can I do now? I know, I'll eat a doughnut instead." Or, "I have spent a whole week without symptoms of genital herpes, I will reward myself with a bar of chocolate." It would seem a bit weird huh? Don't use food or anything else for that matter as a substitute or reward for having stopped smoking!

Something that is always of benefit is exercise. During your life as a smoker you may well have found yourself avoiding physically demanding situations. Break the habit and get moving. Exercise is not simply going down to the gym or running; it's an attitude. Opportunities are always around for exercise: the stairs instead of the lift; parking your car so that you have to walk; walking to the shops instead of taking the car; getting off the bus or underground/subway one or two stops early and walking the rest of the way. Take up dancing, the trampoline, swimming or what ever takes your fancy. Start small and work your way up.

Geoffrey Molloy

17

What about a cigar on special occasions or perhaps a pipe?

The smoking of cigars is perhaps the best example of how the 'monkey see, monkey do' mentality has been exploited by the PR industry on behalf of the tobacco industry. We have been manipulated to perceive the smoking of cigars as being somehow different from and not as dangerous as cigarette smoking. It is also linked to such ideas as success, sophistication, manliness, celebration, and power. The idea about cigar smoking might be expressed like this: smoking cigarettes is something any common pleb might do but cigar smoking is a genuine pleasure, a luxury, somehow more special, sophisticated and elegant. Because you don't inhale the smoke (as much), it is not as addictive or dangerous. It is often portrayed as something that can be done occasionally, like drinking champagne.

Many of the men and some of the women who we see again in our sessions fall for this devious part of the scam. They find themselves at a wedding, baptism or celebrating a major success and they light a cigar, half lying and half hoping that the manipulated mental model − that cigars are different from cigarettes and that you can smoke cigars occasionally − is true, but in a very short time they find themselves smoking the same number of cigarettes as before, or the equivalent in cigars. For those of you reading this book, thinking that cigar or pipe smoking is different, it's wake up time.

First let us get absolutely clear that smoking tobacco in any form is *nicotine addiction,* be it a pipe, cigar, cigarette or mixed with cannabis in a joint; as is chewing anything that contains nicotine.

Remember we are talking about nicotine addiction. Cigar smokers, pipe smokers, tobacco chewers and NRT product users are all addicted to nicotine.

Let's explore the lies and myths around cigar smoking:

First myth — Cigar smoking is safer than smoking cigarettes: A study published in the New England Journal of Medicine states the following:

> One of the main thrusts behind cigars' popularity is the belief that they are a safe alternative to cigarettes because the smoke is not inhaled and because cigars are commonly used only occasionally and not daily. Traditionally, cigar smokers hold the smoke in their mouth and throat, allowing nicotine and other chemical compounds to be absorbed through the mucous lining of the mouth and throat, rather than inhaling the smoke into their lungs.
>
> A smoker can spend more than an hour puffing on a cigar, which has the equivalent risk of oral cancers as smoking a pack of cigarettes a day. Daily cigarette smokers and daily cigar smokers have similar levels of risk for oral cancers. Smokers who smoke more than five cigars per day have lung cancer risks comparable to smoking a pack of cigarettes a day.
>
> The real difference between cigar and cigarette smoking is the type of cancers that cigar smokers develop, which is usually a head or neck cancer, instead of the lung cancer so common among cigarette smokers. Unfortunately, people who switch from using cigarettes to cigars tend to smoke cigars the way they smoked cigarettes: by inhaling deeply and smoking often. Inhalation seems to raise the health risks of cigars so that the smoker will face the same health risks as with cigarette smoking.
>
> Unlike cigarettes, cigars do not have filters to reduce their tar and nicotine content.
>
> The cigar smokers in this study were found to be slightly older, more obese, had higher blood-pressure, higher cholesterol levels and were more likely to have diabetes than non-cigar smokers; also, they consumed more alcohol than non-smokers. Most of them smoked less than 5 cigars a day.
>
> Because of the long aging and fermentation process for cigar leaves, because of the larger size of cigars and because of the toxic way they burn due to cigars' nonporous wrappers, cigar smoke has 20 times more ammonia than cigarettes and 80 to 90 times the number of highly carcinogenic, tobacco-specific nitrosamines. Cigar smoke also contains 30 times more carbon monoxide than cigarette smoke and all of the 4,000 toxic chemical compounds found in cigarette smoke.

126

Why did you start smoking again?

If you believe that smoking cigars is safer than smoking cigarettes, then you have been totally misinformed. Every piece of evidence points to the fact that it is as least as dangerous and in some aspects more dangerous to smoke cigars than to smoke cigarettes.

Second myth – Smoking cigars is less addictive than smoking cigarettes: The following information is sourced from the American Cancer association:

> Cigars and cigarettes differ in both size and the type of tobacco used. Cigarettes are generally more uniform in size and contain less than 1 gram of tobacco each. Cigars, on the other hand, can vary in size and shape and can measure more than 15cm in length. Large cigars can take between 1 and 2 hours to smoke, whereas most cigarettes take less than 10 minutes to smoke. Large cigars typically contain between 5 and 17 grams of tobacco. It is not unusual for some premium cigars to contain the tobacco equivalent of an entire pack of cigarettes.
>
> Cigarettes have an average total nicotine content of about 8.4 milligrams, while many popular brands of cigars will contain between 100 and 200 milligrams, or as much as 450 milligrams of nicotine. In fact, smoking just one large cigar a day will give you more nicotine, more carbon monoxide than smoking a pack of twenty cigarettes.

Third myth – Cigar smoking is sophisticated and elegant: This is the saddest excuse of all. A few years ago I was waiting to meet someone outside the metro/subway station in Moncloa, Madrid. As I sat waiting, I passed the time watching a tramp collecting cigarette-ends (he had about half a dozen big ones). It was a pleasant evening and the tramp sat in the last rays of the evening sun happily slurping from his tetra-brik of Don Simon red wine and smoking his dog-ends. He seemed fairly pleased with himself. As I watched him drugging himself with alcohol and nicotine, I also noticed the disparaging looks he received from the passers-by. I was sure that many of the people that looked at him with distaste used alcohol and tobacco themselves, just as did the tramp. A question entered my head: "So what difference is there between this tramp smoking his fag-ends and drinking from a tetra-brik of red wine and a wealthy man sipping an expensive cognac and smoking a premium cigar?" The answer of course is money. They are both using the same drugs; it's just that one can afford to disguise his addictions better than the other.

Observe people smoking cigars at weddings and other celebrations. The idea of cigar smoking being special and sophisticated is so deep that even non-smoking men, who clearly don't enjoy the experience, will try to smoke a cigar on these occasions. It is their chance to act like a rich man, to celebrate in style even if they end up feeling as sick as a parrot in the process. On these occasions smokers will take the cigar and pretend that they enjoy it, looking for the first opportunity to get rid of it without causing offence.

The whole cigar scam reminds me of the story of the 'Emperor's New Clothes':

A vain emperor of a prosperous city who cared more about clothes than military pursuits or entertainment, hired two swindlers who promise him the finest suit of clothes from the most beautiful cloth. This cloth, they tell him, is invisible to anyone who was either stupid or unfit for his position. The Emperor cannot see the (non-existent) cloth, but pretends that he can for fear of appearing stupid. His ministers do the same. When the swindlers report that the suit is finished, they dress him in mime. The Emperor then goes on a procession through the capital showing off his new 'clothes'. During the course of the procession, a small child cries out, "But he has nothing on!" The crowd realizes the child is telling the truth. The crowd starts to jeer, but the emperor holds his head high and continues the procession.

Let's put this into a modern context: A man is concerned with his outward appearance, his status and pleasure as much as, if not more than, real achievement. The tobacco industry, aided by the PR industry (immoral liars and swindlers to a man) realises this and decides to exploit his weakness. They promise him that all who see him will consider him to be successful, important and handsome if he will just put these brown, smelly things in his mouth, set fire to them and breath in the smoke. They further explain that it is only those people who are stupid, unsophisticated or unsuccessful who are unable to appreciate the fine, cultivated act of breathing in smoke from the brown, smelly thing. The man tries it. It stinks, it makes his eyes water, it burns his throat and even makes him cough. However, he obviously doesn't want to appear stupid or unsophisticated; on the contrary he wants to appear successful, important, powerful and attractive, so he keeps his mouth shut and pretends to like them. After a while he becomes addicted (which was the objective of the swindlers in the first place), but rather than free himself, he joins clubs where he pays a small fortune to be with other sophisticated (read gullible) people who want to learn how to enjoy setting fire to and inhaling smoke from brown, smelly things. Even though all those around him tell him that he is smelly and that he looks stupid with that thing stuck in his face, he ignores them and hangs out with other brown, smelly thing smokers.

Such utter nonsense is talked about cigars and cigar smoking: that it is somehow different, that it is not so addictive and that you can smoke them now and then. Smoking cigars is the opposite of sophisticated. It takes a sophisticated mind to see through the mental manipulation. Any sheep can go along with the fashion. Does the emperor in the story of the emperor's new clothes strike you as being sophisticated, intelligent or attractive? I think not, nor is the cigar smoker. Cigar smoking and pipe smoking are just the same as cigarette smoking and, like all products that cater to our vanity, you pay more to do it.

Geoffrey Molloy

18

The withdrawal is mostly in the mind

Whilst still a smoker, my custom was to relax in the living-room at the end of the day after the children were all in bed and everything was tidied up. I would sit with my wife in companionable silence and read whilst smoking the last cigarettes of the day. I remember on one particular occasion I had only three cigarettes left in the pack I had with me but I wasn't too worried about this, as I knew that I had another full pack on my bedside table. I would have preferred to have two packs spare but accepted the one. I smoked the three cigarettes, then went to our bedroom. Whilst I was preparing for bed, I noted with some relief and satisfaction that the packet of tobacco was on the bedside table, right where I remembered it. I got ready for bed and was close to sleeping, occupying that deliciously strange, relaxed, dreamy state between the waking and sleeping worlds when the thought suddenly struck me, "Better check the pack... just in case." I picked up the pack. It was immediately obvious that something was wrong as the pack was much lighter than it should have been. I opened it and — horror of horrors — found that it was empty! I later discovered that two of my daughters, in a loving attempt to save my life, had stolen my cigarettes and buried them in the garden... but that's another story. My sense of drowsiness evaporated instantly. I tried to relax but it was already 12:30 am and I didn't want to get dressed to go out just to buy tobacco. But after twenty minutes of mental too-ing and fro-ing I got up, got dressed and took the car out to buy tobacco from a filling station 20 minutes drive away. (It was still possible to buy tobacco at filling stations at that time.) When I finally got hold of a couple of packs, I smoked continuously all the way home from the filling station and then another cigarette at home (three or four in total). I finally got to sleep more than an hour later than intended.

You have probably experienced something similar; for example, going down to the local cafeteria in your pyjamas at 01.00 am; or upon returning home from work, always needing to check that you have more than enough tobacco before entering the house for the evening.

These moments of panic or stress are caused not so much by the nicotine withdrawal (I was relaxed and almost asleep – so that clearly wasn't the problem), but by the fear of the possibility of being without my drug. Of course when I lit my cigarette I felt much more relaxed, not realizing that it was the cigarette which made me feel un-relaxed in the first place. A non-smoker would relax without dosing himself up with a nerve-toxin first. It was my belief that I couldn't face the day without a big coffee and my cigarettes and the idea that I might have to do so without cigarettes that provoked the panic.

Get it into your head, smokers don't enjoy smoking. What smokers describe as pleasure or satisfaction is simply the momentary relief they get from the continuous discomfort and suffering of a smoker.

If you believe that you cannot relax without a cigarette then it will be impossible to relax until you have a cigarette. But have you noticed that smoking relaxes you in situations that are relaxing anyway for smokers and non-smokers alike. That special moment at the end of the day, when the kids are finally in bed and you're sitting reading a novel you enjoy, is relaxing whether you are a smoker or not. As a smoker you cannot feel nearly as relaxed as the non-smoker until you have smoked your cigarette and even then you can never entirely eliminate the withdrawal; so a smoker never gets as relaxed as he would if he were a non-smoker. Once again the true effect of smoking is the opposite to what we believe whilst we are addicted.

19

I'd love to be an occasional smoker... just smoke those few 'special ones'

A smoker tries to stop smoking, fails because he says to himself something like, "I can't do this! The rest of my life without a cigarette! I just need my 'special ones'." And so starts the suffering of his attempt to be an occasional smoker. The smoker feels that by smoking less, he will feel less addicted but what happens is that he finds himself thinking constantly about smoking. Whilst our smoker smoked cigarette after cigarette he, like most smokers, smoked automatically, hardly aware that he was smoking. When a smoker smokes without restrictions or control, then the time he is most likely to be aware that he is smoking is when he has smoked too much or has a foul taste in his mouth, or his head aches and he probably feels sick. That is to say, much of his conscious cigarette smoking experience is unpleasant. But now that he is smoking just five a day, each cigarette becomes a prize. But the prize isn't the cigarette; it never has been. Smoking that foul, smelly, carcinogenic thing called a cigarette is what we have to do to relieve the withdrawal, just like eating to relieve hunger or drinking water to relieve thirst. The longer you wait, the greater the need and thus the greater the relief.

The difference between hunger and thirst, on the one hand and nicotine withdrawal on the other, is that hunger and thirst are part of our survival mechanism. Hunger and thirst exist to ensure that we provide our bodies with vital materials to keep us alive. When we do so, we experience relief which we recognise as pleasure. Nicotine withdrawal feels something like hunger but it is not hunger for food but for a nerve-toxin, that brings in its wake sickness, slavery and death. Poisoning yourself simply is not pleasurable. How can it be? It is the nicotine parasite trying to feed itself. Stop feeding it and you put an end to the hunger. The parasite dies and you are free.

Remember, the determining factors in the number of cigarettes that any smoker smokes are the same as for any drug addiction: the physical capacity of your body to withstand the systematic poisoning and the opportunity to do so. If it were any different, it wouldn't be drug addiction would it?

Time and again smokers stop smoking and instead of celebrating, they start whining and pining for just one cigarette, just those special ones. They simply don't exist. 'Just that one cigarette' means the *life of a smoker* – lack of energy, bad breath, headache, slavery, fear, social stigma, feeling of stupidity, coughing, sickness and disease. There is nothing else, all of this suffering to achieve what? Nothing. All of this just to try and relieve the discomfort caused by the previous cigarette.

What smokers are wishing for in these situations is something that they themselves don't want. All that really exists is the life of a smoker, the life of a nicotine addict. The reason they stopped smoking was because they hated living the life of a smoker. Now they are feeling miserable because they cannot have something that they themselves don't want.

Is that a recipe for misery and failure or what? The person who thinks like that will feel miserable if he cannot smoke just one cigarette but will feel even worse if he does light one and finds himself once again with the only reality there is – the depression, sickness and slavery of the life of a smoker.

The utter pointlessness is mind-boggling: to feel unhappy for the loss of something that you yourself don't want. Think what this means. Whilst you cannot smoke, you will feel miserable (because you cannot have just one – something that doesn't exist anyway). And if you do smoke one, then you will soon feel depressed when you realise that you are hooked once again.

This is all especially heart breaking because stopping smoking, in reality, is wonderful. How could it not be? There is absolute nothing to give up or sacrifice. In fact it is just the opposite. You are giving yourself more money, more energy, greater peace of mind, more vitality, greater freedom, self-respect. There is nothing to give up. You're not sacrificing anything because there is nothing to sacrifice.

When I meet smokers and ex-smokers socially, they will often tell me their own smoking history. Most of the ex-smokers I speak to, understand that there is no such thing as just one cigarette. However, many still feel that they have sacrificed something, which is sad because they are in reality free but ironically they don't know it. Even if they have a sense of sacrifice, they realise that they are much better off as a non-smoker than they ever were as a smoker. The funniest ones in these situations are the smokers who try to convince me that they have it controlled, that they love smoking and that they can stop smoking whenever they want, even pointing out the fact that they stopped smoking last year for a few months, without being able to see the contradiction. If they love smoking so much, why did they stop? One smoker claimed that he was previously a heavy smoker but now only smoked five a day. When I pointed out to him that he had already smoked more than five during our conversation, he told me parties were different. It's always different isn't it?

The fact is that all drug addicts lie − to others (especially those closest to them) and most importantly to themselves. A man in our village, a neighbour and a former heavy smoker had stopped smoking for more than a year when I saw him at the annual village 'fiesta', smoking a cigarette. I said, "I see that you've started smoking again." He denied this, in spite of the fact that he had a lighted cigarette in his mouth. He went on to explain that he was only smoking on that particular day as it was the annual village fiesta. It seemed a rum sort of excuse but I didn't comment further. A few months later there he was smoking at another village event. He explained that since he hadn't got hooked, he was now smoking just at fiestas. I didn't press the point. Some weeks later, as I walked past his farm I heard him shouting out to his wife, "Did you buy my cigarettes then?" I fully expected that the next time I saw him he would be back to smoking two packs a day. But no, every time we met, he claimed he wasn't smoking. I finally caught him walking along a country lane in a cloud of smoke. Now, who he was trying to fool isn't clear − just me, his friends, his neighbours? My feeling is that he was mostly trying to fool himself. Haven't we all been guilty of similar self-deception at some time?

Geoffrey Molloy

20
Curiosity killed the cat

Amongst the saddest cases I see in our back-up sessions are those who start again out of curiosity. These people have often spent years without smoking. They are very happy as non-smokers. They don't miss them, nor do they believe that there are any benefits in smoking. However, they, like you and me, remain subjected to the scheming of the tobacco and PR industry which continue to bombard us with their lies in any way available.

Our happy non-smoker finds himself in a social situation, for example, a wedding. The cigars are passed out as part of the celebrations. He might at first refuse but perhaps curiosity gets the better of him. He has recovered from the effects of smoking and has never felt so healthy in his life. But this feeling of great health, which just a few years ago, was something to be marvelled at, is now taken for granted. He is curious: "I haven't smoked a cigar in years... I wonder if they taste as horrible as I remember, although perhaps I'd better not because I might start smoking again. Still, I've spent three, five, ten or however long years without smoking and it's been easy. I've faced and overcome all types of situations without smoking — social ones and stressful ones. I've got smoking under control. Surely no harm can come from smoking just one cigar. After all it's just one cigar and only here, at this wedding." He smokes his cigar which tastes horrible and then what happens? There is now a subtle change in attitude. Instead of being a smoker who wants to be non-smoker, he now becomes an ex-smoker who is trying to figure out how to be an occasional smoker. For years, the idea of smoking simply did not occur to our man, but now there is a little voice that suggests every so often the idea of smoking another cigar but only on 'special occasions'.

A week goes by or maybe several weeks and the man now finds himself in another 'cigar situation': Saturday night after dinner, for example. Dinner finishes and the cigars come out and he thinks, "Well, I smoked one before and I didn't get hooked, so what harm can a single cigar on a Saturday night do? It's not as if I'm going back to smoking cigarettes!" What he hasn't asked himself is the key question: "Why, if the first one was so horrible, do I want to light another one?"

Our man wants to believe that he can control it (although nothing could be further from the truth), so he will use all the facts he can muster as evidence that he has it under control

He might maintain this 'just one cigar on Saturday night' thing for a few weeks or even longer. During this time he is growing in confidence as he is collecting evidence that this time, "It *is* different, this time I *do* have it controlled." He might now negotiate a deal with himself, which he does by saying something like, "Well, I've managed not to get hooked." (Who's he kidding?) "That means I can smoke just, say three special cigarettes a day, perhaps one with my coffee in the morning, another after lunch and maybe one in the evening." He might be aware at this point that apart from the little voice that is constantly saying, "You're doing all right, you *really* have got it controlled this time," there is another voice which is saying something like, "You prat! What have you done!?"

The smoker might manage with his three-a-day thing for a while, perhaps days or weeks, but sooner or later he finds himself on a night out and smokes twenty cigarettes or maybe 5 cigars and now he starts 'double accounting'. He tells himself, "Those cigarettes or cigars that I smoked at the party simply don't count because I still *really* only smoke three a day." He renegotiates his agreement with himself and thinks, "Well, I will smoke three cigars a day except in those special, social situations, like when I'm out drinking." Things start to get ridiculous now as he realises he is arranging his life so that he is out drinking as frequently as possible. It doesn't matter whether he goes back to smoking the same (or even more) as before, straightaway or whether he falls back slowly; the fact is that he is once again hooked.

These smokers, when they appear in our back-up sessions are usually very angry with themselves; angry at how stupidly they threw away their freedom for a lie, and got in return something that they themselves hoped they would never have again.

21

Obsession and the fear of failure

Strong-willed people are accustomed to achieving things by applying their will. When confronted with any task or problem, they look for things to *DO:* the right tools, the words, phrases, tricks to achieve their goal. They come to the session, stop smoking and everything is fine and dandy. However, their fear of failure is great. Time goes by. They haven't smoked but they feel that they have to keep their guard up. They believe that if they don't do this, they might start smoking again. They, like many people, believe that in order to achieve anything worthwhile, they must *do something,* make an *effort, force* themselves, *work* at it. They stop smoking and instead of accepting their decision and thinking, "Brilliant! thank God I'm free, thank God I don't have to do that anymore," and getting on with their lives, they stand guard on their actions and most of all, their thoughts, looking for any sign that things aren't as they *should* be. They feel that they have to make sure that things are 'going well'.

This whole idea of monitoring and keeping vigil on your thoughts is rather like a cat taking up position outside a mouse-hole all day long and *hoping not to see a mouse.* There is no more likely place to see the mouse. One day our ex-smoker finds himself in a situation in which, for many years, he smoked (drinks with friends for example, or an argument with his partner) and the thought, "I want a cigarette," springs into his mind. The thought is perfectly natural. Think for a moment. After so many years smoking in every possible situation, it would frankly be weird not to have such a thought every now and then. It is possible that the strong-willed person will start to obsess and think something like, "I shouldn't still be thinking like this! I should have forgotten about it by now. I shouldn't want to smoke! My God, I'm going to have to watch out, I'm obviously still not free! I know, I'll try to distract myself from this thought. I'll try to keep myself busy. Oh I wish I didn't want a cigarette. I'll try not to think about it..." Of course, the very moment that you try not to think about something is when you ensure that you cannot think of anything else. The person goes through a hellish internal yes/no fight, generating stress and often anxiety until he reaches the point when he thinks, "I cannot stand any more of this! I don't want to smoke but I need to find some peace. I simply cannot live with this stress, this torture."

Staying as a non-smoker requires no effort at all. It is not about doing anything; it is about Acceptance: accepting the evidence and accepting your decision.

I am sure that if you are reading this book that you have experienced some of what I've described.

But when will I be free?

Ask yourself the question, at what point does a smoker free herself of her addiction? When can she say, "Brilliant, I'm free, I'm a non-smoker"? For most smokers the answer that springs to mind is, "Never. Once a smoker always a smoker!"

Implicit in the mental model above is that there is some sort of genuine pleasure in smoking and that you, being the poor addict that you are, will never (unlike a normal person) be able to enjoy the pleasure of smoking again, not even one cigarette (even though we have seen that there is no genuine pleasure to smoking, that there is no such thing as smoking just one cigarette and that there never was). Why not? Because according to the nonsensical model, touted by many 'experts', it's genetic, it's your personality. What utter rubbish! This idea is also propagated by organisations such as AA. It is the message of doom, the message of 'you were born a nicotine addict; you will always be a nicotine addict; it is your fate; you have an addictive personality, addictive genes'. (Even though there is *no* scientific proof for either of these ideas).

I stopped smoking eighteen years ago. I have been free and felt free for these eighteen years. Smoking is an addiction to nicotine. The effect of regularly taking any addictive drug is to make you into an addict of that drug. If you and I were to start regularly taking heroin then – guess what? – we would become heroin addicts. The addiction is in the drug, not in the person.

I remember watching the film 'Titanic' and the heart-breaking scene as the character played by Leonardo di Caprio, as well as many others, died of hypothermia in the cold Atlantic sea. All of those passengers unfortunate enough to spend that night in the sea, died. Now imagine if the subsequent investigation found that all of those passengers that died in the freezing Atlantic suffered from an 'easily-dies-of-hypothermia personality', it would have been greeted with outrage.

The problem is that if you continue to believe that you can never be free, then you will never be free. Not so long ago, a young lady of twenty three came to a session. We calculated that if she stopped smoking (which she did), she could reasonably expect to live another 70 years. That girl is free; she stopped and is now delighted with life as a non-smoker. Imagine if after the session she continued to believe she could never be free. That belief would mean that she would spend the rest of her life (70 years or so) frightened of failure, waiting or even obsessing about possible failure, even though – and here's the good part – she never smoked another cigarette. That would be so sad and utterly pointless. Imagine her at 90, having lived a wonderful, productive life, peacefully lying on her death bed with her children and grandchildren all around her. It is clear that she does not have much time left and one of her grandchildren says to her, "Grandma you were a real non-smoker after all." Imagine if Grandma replied, "Not so fast! I reckon that I've a few more hours left. I might still smoke… You never know."

The reality is that she freed herself in the moment that she made her decision to put out her last cigarette. She is out of the quagmire of nicotine addiction and happy to be free. She is happy because she sees the scam for what it is. She does not worry that she might have a 'sinks-into-quagmire' personality or genes.

Geoffrey Molloy

22

Doubt and hope

I live in a mountainous region of Cantabria in the north of Spain. One of the things that we enjoy doing is walking or riding in what is called here the 'monte'. The monte around our home is truly beautiful and generally safe if you understand the country and follow a few simple rules. One of the hazards here is what is known locally as a 'lamiza'. In this context the word refers to a geographic feature which can be lethal. It tends to occur in shallow gullies between hills. Because of the shallow slope, the surface water and silt from higher up tend to pool forming a 'lamiza'. I haven't found a direct translation for this word. The closest that I can come up with is quagmire. This quagmire can be lethal to any animal that tries to cross it. It is made even more treacherous because, at first glance, it appears not much different from the firm ground surrounding it. In fact, to the experienced eye, the quagmire can be detected by a subtle change in vegetation. Each year a number of young animals (foals for example) will make the mistake of entering these quagmires, often with fatal consequences.

Such a quagmire is dangerous to you or any creature that has the bad luck to try and cross it. It does not depend on your personality, genes or will-power. You will sink. Such is the nature of this quagmire. It always was and always will be.

Now imagine that whilst still a youngster, someone that could only be described as both manipulative and deeply evil, convinces you that you won't really be adult, you cannot really be cool until you've 'walked the quagmire'. Even though others have warned of the dangers, this evil, psychopathic manipulator speaks in seductive tones and through his extensive experience knows exactly how to manipulate you. You are finally persuaded and such is the skill of this evil psychopath that you even believe that it's your own idea. You start walking over it and at first think, "I don't know what all the fuss is about. This isn't so difficult!" Then you find yourself stuck but you are not worried as you believe that you can free yourself whenever you want, although you start to believe that it's probably going to be difficult to get out without sacrificing a shoe. Now something sinister starts to happen: you feel yourself sinking

143

ever so slowly. Perhaps you now realise that you are in trouble. You struggle and find that you only sink faster. You shout for help. A passing tourist, who also happens to be a healer, comes to your aid but all he does is berate you, telling you that you are in a very dangerous situation and that you should get out as soon as possible. You feel mind-bogglingly frustrated. You already know that! The absolute last thing you need right now is some nitwit frightening you even more with his graphic horror stories of the fate of those who didn't manage to escape. Fortunately for you, there comes along a local chap who, although not a healer, has many years of experience in rescuing people and animals from the clutches of the quagmire. He explains that first you need to stop struggling. Then he explains what is happening and pulls you out.

Smoking is like a quagmire. It is a problem for anyone who falls in, irrespective of their genes or personality. It is the nature of the smoking quagmire. Always was and always will be. Anyone who has the bad luck to fall into a quagmire will find themselves sinking. Once you realise the nature of a quagmire and the danger it represents, you don't need anyone to tell you not to walk on it again. The smoking scam and its mental manipulation mean that we doubt the evidence of our own flesh. We believe that somehow we are weak, that we are at fault and that there are people somewhere who can walk on quagmires, aren't affected by them and actually find it a real pleasure to do so. We doubt ourselves. The smoker lives in the hope that one day he will find the trick to walking the quagmire. *IT IS NOT POSSIBLE – it is the very nature of the quagmire that makes it impossible.* But whilst he believes it must be possible, then he will also believe that the problem is in him and not in the nature of quagmires. The smoker might think something like, "If only I can find a way to change myself, to do it differently, then it must be possible."

In truth, the smoker frees himself once he accepts the reality that he doesn't enjoy being a smoker; that there is nothing to give up; that there is no such thing as one cigarette, putting out his last cigarette and deciding to enjoy his decision.

I was once convinced that I could never be free. I had seen my father and a good friend die of smoking related diseases and yet I still smoked. This all changed for me when I realised and accepted the truth: that there really is absolutely nothing to give up, nothing to sacrifice. From that moment onwards I knew that it was possible to be free. Many smokers say, "Well, OK, I understand that, but tell me, when will I feel like a non-smoker?"

23

OK, so when will I feel like a non-smoker?

One of the difficult things for a smoker to do is to imagine how it will feel to be a non-smoker. Before I stopped smoking I was in the same position as many. I started smoking whilst still no more than a child and stopped when I was thirty-five. Up to the moment in which I did finally stop smoking and free myself, I had never been an adult or adolescent non-smoker. It was something outside of my experience. That goes for most smokers. Most of us have been smoking for so long that we simply cannot imagine life as a non-smoker. In this sense, smokers and non-smokers do not feel any different.

The fact is that you remain the same person and thus you feel the same. I admit there are some differences, like having more energy, greater peace of mind, more vitality; feeling more relaxed, less stressed; things taste and smell better; *you* smell better, you have better concentration, feel more positive and better able to face life's difficulties. Perhaps the best of all is the marvellous sense of freedom, but you still feel like the same person.

If at any time you want to see me vomit, feed me tinned pilchards. I hate tinned pilchards. They are a guaranteed way to make me throw up. So, if you were to ask me how I feel not eating pilchards, I would have to say, "Great, normal!" Not that I spend much time thinking about eating or not eating them. However, if by contrast, tinned pilchards were my favourite food, if I loved eating pilchards above all other foods but you prohibited me from doing so and then asked me how I feel, I would feel bad because I would feel that I was being prohibited from doing something that I enjoy.

There we have it. It isn't the physical nicotine withdrawal that causes the problem; it is the feeling that we are being denied something that we desire. Now with tinned pilchards or some other food, this might be understandable. But with smoking there is no sense at all, as there is no genuine benefit or pleasure. So if you decide to stop smoking and then start whining and pining, then in reality you are simply feeling bad because you cannot have something that you yourself don't want. How utterly pointless! With that attitude you cannot win. If you don't smoke you'll feel sad because you're absurdly wishing for something that doesn't exist; and if you do smoke, you'll feel even worse because you will quickly find yourself back with the only reality there ever was or will be: the depressing slavery of nicotine addiction.

Think for a moment. Is there anything so pathetic as feeling sad because you cannot have something that you yourself don't want. I think the most intelligent and realistic point of view is that you are in fact freeing yourself of an awful disease. This is a cause for celebration, not sadness; celebration, not just in the moment in which you free yourself but for the rest of your life.

And that is the great advantage of deciding to no longer be a slave of the tobacco industry, deciding to stop spending vast sums of your money to systematically poison and destroy yourself.

Remember it is not the physical nicotine withdrawal that causes the problem. It never was. It is the idea that you are being forced to sacrifice something. In fact the opposite is happening. You are giving yourself one of the best presents you could possibly imagine. You are freeing yourself of a horrible disease. You will achieve what all smokers want to achieve: FREEDOM.

24

Choosing the best moment to stop

I stopped smoking during what was one of the most stressful periods of my life. I didn't plan it that way but that's how it happened. In a strange way and contrary to what is generally believed, I found that it was the best time to stop smoking. Many clients have a similar experience. They have told me how stopping smoking right in the middle of one of life's stressful episodes left them with a marvellous sense of confidence. They felt that having got through that difficult situation without smoking gave them the feeling of certainty that they were truly free.

Whilst we smoke we are being pulled in one direction by fearful thoughts which call to us to stop, thoughts like, "It's killing me," "It's turned me into a slave," "It's costing me a fortune," "It's going to give me some horrible disease." At the same time we have the other fear-driven thoughts like, "How am I going to enjoy myself, face life, socialise, concentrate, relax?" etc. For most of a smoker's life his fear of stopping outweighs the fear of carrying on, so he keeps on smoking.

What you need to successfully stop smoking is the correct state of mind. That state of mind is not, "Well, I've got to stop because... it's bad, for my children," etc... nor because "the disadvantages clearly outweigh the advantages, therefore I'm going to stop."

The correct attitude is: "I don't want to smoke anymore as there is simply no point to it. How wonderful that I don't have to anymore!"

I often receive calls from smokers thinking about stopping smoking who, before booking their place ask questions such as, "Should I stop before or after my holidays?" or "I'm going through a difficult time at the moment, perhaps I should wait until I am free of stress?" These questions are asked either to improve the chances of success or to confirm to her/his husband/wife (who is pressuring them to stop) that this is not a good moment. The root cause of these questions is the same: the manipulated mental map.

147

This is easier to grasp if you substitute the word cigarette for mango. Let's say that you have discovered that, for whatever reason, mangoes provoke a painful and dangerous reaction in your body. There is a 50% chance that this reaction could be fatal at some time in the future. As much as you enjoy the taste of mangoes, you decide that you no longer want to eat them. When would you stop eating them? In the New Year? After your holidays? Would you wait for a better moment? Would you wait until your fortieth birthday? Would your decision depend on the price of mangoes? Or, best of all, perhaps you would wait for World Anti-Mango day. Of course not, you would do it straight away!

The dates smokers choose for stopping smoking are often event driven. Here are some examples of events that may drive a smoker to stop:

A shocking event: The smoker is diagnosed with a smoking related disease or receives news of the death of a friend or of a colleague diagnosed with a terminal smoking related disease such as cancer.

Other event: Birth of a child, sick child (for example with asthma), getting married, getting divorced, pressure to stop smoking from family members (usually spouse or parents), holidays or a promise.

Make-believe special date: New Year's day, birthday, saints day, World Tobacco day are examples of the most common make-believe dates.

Shocking or strong events might seem like a good time to stop. The shocking event (death of a friend from smoking or finding out that you yourself are diagnosed with a dangerous smoking related disease) changes the balance of fear for a while. The fear of carrying on smoking becomes stronger than the fear of stopping smoking and the smoker decides to stop. His motivation is strong. However, he continues to feel that smoking does provide him with some genuine benefit or pleasure. Usually within weeks, the event or symptoms that changed the balance of fear have weakened. The death of the friend simply isn't as vivid as it was. It no longer has such power to shock or frighten. Perhaps it was the diagnosis of a threatening smoking related disease which provided the motivation. Once the body starts eliminating the nerve toxin nicotine and the other 4,000 toxic compounds, the smoker feels much better. As the symptoms start to ease off so does his motivation. Such is human nature.

Some smokers feel that if only the doctor would say something to them; if only they were just ordered by their doctor to stop smoking, then they would do so. It is just another excuse. Think again of the mangoes. If you knew that they were toxic, carcinogenic, destroying your health, costing you a fortune and giving you bad breath, making you age prematurely, would you really adopt the attitude, "I will stop when the doctor tells me to"? Of course you wouldn't! In fact, try to imagine convincing anyone that such an attitude is logical, everyone would think that you were a complete prat – you most of all.

It is often the clients who have already been diagnosed with a killer disease that have to work hardest to stop, simply because they are in a constant state of panic. Think for a moment. What keeps us smoking? It is trying to fill the void – the void caused by nicotine. To discover that you have a killer disease provokes fear and even panic. This makes the void appear even greater, Thus your need for the cause of your disease (smoking) seems greater. The thing you feel you need most to help you is the very thing that you are not allowed to do which creates both fear and panic. It is difficult to learn when you are in a state of panic and fear.

Some time ago, two middle-aged sisters appeared in a session; they obviously took pride in their appearance. Within a few minutes of entering, one (let us call her Liz) started to say that this probably wouldn't work for her; that she already understood the arguments but simply loved smoking; that for her, smoking truly was a friend, a pleasure. During the session her sister (let us call her Mary) admitted to being in the session because she had been diagnosed with emphysema and 'had to' stop smoking. Liz then explained to us all that she was really only there in the session to support her sister. At the end of the session Mary seemed very happy with her decision. Her expression had changed during the session from one of stress and anxiety to an expression of joy and confidence. I felt very pleased for her. She sent me a message a few days later just to say how marvellous she felt to be free of her addiction. A few more days passed and she telephoned to tell me that now she was finding it difficult. Although she didn't say it directly (her sister was close by), she explained that her sister was telling her (in the nicest possible way) that she wasn't really free; that although it had been easy at the beginning, it would become more difficult and other things which seem designed to pressure her to start again. My gut reaction was anger at Liz for doing what seemed to me something quite awful. They both came to a back-up session as they both had started smoking again. It was after this back-up session that we discovered that Liz in fact, had already been diagnosed with lung and bladder cancer (classic smoking related cancers). These were salient facts which she had neglected to mention in the first session.

This story illustrates several points. Liz had cancer but that knowledge didn't help her stop. In fact, I have met few people with such powers of self-delusion. She continued to swear that she loved smoking and that irrespective of what anyone said, it was a pleasure. When her sister Mary realised that she was not sacrificing anything, Liz set about undermining her confidence and getting her to smoke once again. So not only did she herself not stop, she tried to drag someone else down with her. You may be thinking, "What a cow! How evil!" I don't believe that she was a cow or evil but beneath her controlled, attractive exterior was a raging panic and desperation which undermined her ability to simply listen, hear and learn. She had clung on to the story that it didn't affect her and that she loved smoking for so many years. She clutched at this argument to save her pride as a drowning man may clutch at a straw. How difficult would it be for anyone to learn anything in such a state!

Some do have the ability to put their fears to one side and learn; others don't. Many of their faces are clearly burnt into our memories.

Hoping that an external event can provide you with the motivation is not very successful either. If your objective is to free yourself for good of the slavery of nicotine addiction, then it cannot depend on any external circumstance. The motivation is liable to evaporate as external circumstances will always change. What seemed like a good reason to stop yesterday can become the opposite very quickly. For example: "I must stop for my son's asthma," changes a few years later to, "My son no longer has asthma which means I can now smoke!" How about, "I'll stop smoking to please my girlfriend"? This can quickly change to, "My new girlfriend smokes and if I want to get on well with her it would be better if I smoked too".

Finally we have the make-believe date. Why make-believe? Because the date has absolutely nothing to do with your addiction. Whilst stopping in response to an external event is not ideal, it at least has the benefit of boosting your motivation. Picking a make-believe date, no matter how significant it might be in other areas of your life, offers little in the way of advantage and many disadvantages and can easily work against you. Another problem with make-believe dates is that they often are used simply as excuses to keep postponing the attempt. The life of a smoker is typically one missed date after another: New Year, Easter, back to work after Easter, summer holidays, after summer holidays, birthday, Christmas, New Year and so it goes on.

Another problem with make-believe dates is that they are often the worse time to stop. Two examples: "I believe that I am a stress smoker so I will stop when I go on my summer holidays." Many smokers start well at the beginning of their holiday. After a week they think, "This is great, I can manage without smoking." After two weeks, they think, "Wow! I'm doing all right here. During week three they start to think,

Why did you start smoking again?

"Well, I'm doing all right but I don't know how I'll manage when I get back to work. It's going to be difficult." As he ruminates, the smoker becomes increasingly anxious as he starts imagining how difficult it's going to be. He thinks something like, "A non-smoker on holiday is one thing but a non-smoker at work is something else entirely." The more he thinks about working without smoking, the more anxious he becomes. Finally, he thinks, "This stopping smoking business is ruining what's left of my holiday. Better that I start smoking now and avoid further pain as I'm probably going to start again anyway." He starts smoking before getting anywhere near the office. Even if our smoker manages to stay stopped until he gets back to work, going back to work for many people is a real low point of the year. The better the holiday, the more stressed we will feel having to return to work.

The next example is one of the true favourites: New Year. Most smokers have tried stopping smoking on New Year's Eve. There is probably not a worse moment to stop smoking, You have probably spent days eating, drinking and smoking far too much. You probably feel that you simply don't want to smoke anymore, not because your will or determination is particularly developed at the beginning of the year but because you are smoked out. (Many smokers go through the same thing if they smoke and drink a lot on Saturday night. Sunday morning they don't smoke because it makes them feel sick.) The determination soon wears off and the person then has to get back to work where he finds himself with other recent quitters. No one feels very thrilled at returning to work. The tobacco companies make a special effort around these dates using PR to keep you hooked. At work and socially you are surrounded by a lot of irritable ex-smokers, trying to cope without their cigarette too. Most feel that they are having a hard time of it. Inevitably, they start to fall back. As one falls back, he tries to drag down others too, freely offering cigarettes, trying to make it easier for you to smoke. Some are successful but the odds are against you.

So when is the best time to stop?

If you have been following the arguments and instructions, you will have realised that the most important aspect of getting free of your nicotine addiction is your attitude. To be successful your attitude should be: I don't smoke anymore as there is no point; there are simply no benefits; there is absolutely nothing to give up. What a relief not to have to poison myself anymore with that disgusting nerve toxin. I'm free. Brilliant!

Bring to your mind one of your children, your parents or your spouse — someone close and dear to you. Imagine that they have been diagnosed with a terrible disease that is destroying their quality of life, making them nervous, unhappy; they also smell bad and have less and less stamina and vitality. Fortunately there is a quick and rapid cure. What would your advice be? Would you advise them to wait until the New Year, their 40th birthday or after the summer holidays to get cured. Of course not! You'd want to see them free as soon as possible.

So when is the best moment to stop smoking?

It is now, today. There is no other logical moment. There is no better moment.

25

The right frame of mind

If you have read and understood this book, then you are well prepared to stop smoking. Just follow the instructions from here on in. If you feel a bit nervous, don't worry about it. It's completely understandable. Remember, it is very easy to confuse excitement with fear. Check to see if you also feel excited. Don't delay. If you feel that you want to delay and choose a make-believe or any other date, it means that you haven't understood the whole message. Get back and re-read the relevant bit until you are confident that you've got it right.

Why should you delay? There is absolutely nothing to give up; there is nothing to sacrifice; cigarettes have never given you anything except prolonged suffering. Cigarettes turned you into that dog chewing on the sharp bone. The thing that you thought filled the emptiness has all this time been the principal cause of that feeling. If at any time you feel like dancing for joy to celebrate your freedom, do it! You will be giving yourself the best gift ever. You are giving yourself more energy, vitality, greater peace of mind, less stress, more freedom; you will smell better. You will feel soooo much better about yourself; you will have a happier and healthier life.

Or as a lovely lady client said to me, "You must be mad if you feel anything but a sense of joy when you stop smoking." I agree with her completely.

Write your own script

The wonderful benefit of stopping smoking is Freedom. People often talk about the physical and financial benefits. The biggest benefits, however, are mental and spiritual – freedom from the grinding bondage of drug addiction. Whilst you are a nicotine addict, every aspect of your life is conditioned by your addiction. You must have your drug! If you cannot smoke somewhere, then you would rather not go. You spend your life living out the script that the tobacco industry wrote and burned into your mind, the script which keeps you living in fear – a slave spending a fortune to destroy yourself.

Soon you will be free. Now as your own script writer, what will you do with that power, with that freedom? There are three basic scripts available to you. The first two are the scripts given to you by the tobacco industry. These are:

1. **Bondage and suffering:** Keep right on smoking. Condemn yourself to a life of fear, sickness and bondage to nicotine, a slave to the tobacco industry. Is that what you want? NO… It's what the tobacco industry wants. That's why you read this book in the first place.

2. **I wish I could smoke just one but I can't:** Don't smoke but feel deprived, feel miserable: You stop smoking but without accepting the reality that there is absolutely nothing to sacrifice. You keep hoping that some day you might just smoke one cigarette or cigar. *But there is no such thing; there never was.* That's the illusion that got you hooked in the first place. It means that even though you aren't smoking, you will never feel free. You will spend your life feeling sad, whining and pining because you cannot have something that you yourself don't want. Pathetic! Is that what you want? NO… It's what the tobacco industry wants.

3. **Brilliant I'm so happy to be free!** *You write your own script.* You decide to free yourself permanently and you enjoy your decision, your freedom, not just today but for the rest of your life. There is nothing bad happening here. You are achieving not just what you want to achieve but what every smoker on the planet would love to achieve. **Freedom!** There is absolutely nothing to sacrifice, nothing to give up. In fact you are doing the opposite; you are giving yourself a wonderful present: a longer, healthier, happier life. The good moments will be better and the bad moments not so bad. You will have more energy, look better, smell better, feel less stressed, feel more confident but most importantly, you will have more self-respect. Smoking will just seem like a bad dream. You won't envy smokers but look upon them with compassion. You will realise that smokers are envious of you. Is that the script you want? I am sure that it is. So when you make your decision and choose your script consciously, make sure that it is the right one.

Why would you choose anything but script number three?

You never decided to become a smoker. Both as a child and adult you have been manipulated by the evil scum that run the tobacco industry and the PR industry – their cynical, immoral helpers. You were seduced into trying an experimental cigarette. You had no idea that it was all a scam, that you were introducing a type of parasite into your body, a tapeworm that feeds on nicotine. When you lit that first cigarette you set off a chain reaction which led to the thousands upon thousands of cigarettes that you have smoked since then. If only you had known then what you know about smoking now, would you ever have lit that first cigarette? Of course not! When you lit that first cigarette you brought the horror of drug addiction into your life. Slowly, almost imperceptibly, you lost your peace of mind and replaced it with fear, lethargy, depression, stress, bad breath, premature ageing, wheezing, coughing, lies and self-deceit constantly undermining your self-respect.

No one enjoys being a smoker. The next time you find yourself at a social occasion, take the opportunity to observe the 'five a day casual smokers smoking like their life depended on it. If you draw their attention to the fact that they are smoking compulsively, they will tell you, "Parties are different," or "It's a 'special occasion," or "These cigarettes don't count because I 'really' only smoke five a day." Watch them! They don't feel happier than the non smokers; it's just that they feel that they cannot face or enjoy life without their drug. Most of the time they don't even know that they're smoking; its automatic, compulsive, and unconscious.

All drug addicts lie to other people but most of all to themselves. But no matter how they try to deceive themselves, when they wake up in the morning they are smokers, nicotine addicts. They have to keep right on smoking, in spite of the fear of cancer, the smell, the lethargy, their grey complexions, the stress, the pain they cause to their families, the wasted money, the feeling of stupidity, the depression, the social stigma — trying with ever increasing desperation to get back to the peace of mind they had before they started smoking. The only thing that stops them is the next cigarette. And what do they get in return for their money, suffering and depression? Nothing, not a single genuine benefit!

So don't envy smokers. Either openly or in secret, they will be envying you. You wouldn't envy a heroin or cocaine addict would you? Of course not! It's not heroin that kills 14,000 people a day; it's nicotine.

Like any drug addiction, it simply isn't going to get better or disappear on its own. Like any addiction, it will keep deteriorating until your life becomes a desperate living nightmare. Think! If you don't enjoy being a smoker today, you will enjoy it even less tomorrow and the day after that and the day after that. So from today do not envy smokers, treat them with compassion. Think, "There but for the grace of God go I."

Geoffrey Molloy

26
Decision Time

If you have read this book, understood the ideas and followed the instructions, you will be ready to take your decision. Allow yourself to feel excited about your decision, your freedom.

If you are feeling nervous, accept it. Maybe it has suddenly dawned on you that you are really going to stop smoking for good, that you are finally freeing yourself. Think, almost every important step, change or achievement in life brings with it both fear and excitement.

Maybe you have noticed a flicker of doubt when you think of the rest of your life without smoking another cigarette. So just get really clear that the only alternative that you have is to keep right on smoking, never being allowed to stop. It's simple. You have smoked thousands of cigarettes and on the basis of that extensive experience, you realise it is slavery and that you simply don't want to do it anymore.

It's your decision: First of all remember that it is your decision and no one else's. You are taking this decision not because you *have to stop smoking* but because you *want to*.

This is not an attempt to stop smoking: *Just do it!* If you decide that you are going to *try* to stop smoking or you are going to *attempt* to stop smoking, then that is exactly what you will achieve. You get what you decide. You will try and the result will be just another 'attempt'. You are not trying or attempting, you are stopping definitely.

No conditions and no negotiation: A common mistake in making the decision is to put conditions on it. For example, "I am a non-smoker but God knows what I'll do if I start to get fat," or "I am a non-smoker but God knows what I'll do if I cannot concentrate." By imposing such conditions, you will be taking not one decision but two: the decision to stop smoking and the decision to start again. What a waste of time, energy and effort!

Your Decision

Now is a good moment to light your last cigarette. (If you have already stopped smoking DO NOT LIGHT A CIGARETTE). The attitude you should adopt for taking the decision is not: "I must never smoke again." See it as it really is: "Thank God that I no longer have to put these filthy, carcinogenic, smelly things in my mouth and set fire to them. I'm free... how wonderful!"

Now when you take your decision you commit to becoming a non-smoker. When you put out that last cigarette, you become a non- smoker.

As I wrote earlier what we are looking for is a certain attitude. That attitude should include certain very clear ideas:

1. Understand and accept that you do not enjoy being a smoker, a nicotine addict. You never have and you never will. I don't mean that intellectually you understand the arguments but don't understand why you feel that you do enjoy an 'occasional cigarette'. There is no such thing as an occasional cigarette. Just the awful reality, the life and suffering of a nicotine addict. Like millions of others, you fell into nicotine addiction through smoking those experimental cigarettes and now, just like millions before you, you are about to escape. You didn't ever decide to become a smoker. The reason that you picked up this book in the first place is that you are tired of smoking hour after hour, day after day, year after year, never being allowed to stop. You started because you were conned like so many youngsters into seeing the illusion of 'just one cigarette'. If you had only known then what you know now, would you have ever lit that first cigarette? Of course not!!!!!! Instead of just one cigarette what you got was the life of a nicotine addict, the life of a smoker and all the suffering that it implies: coughing, wheezing, lack of energy, lack of vitality, the social stigma, being despised by other people, the stink, the slavery, the fear, the depression; the sense of stupidity of spending your hard earned money simply to systematically poison yourself. All of this for what? To get back to feeling as well as you did before you started. What's the only thing that's stopping you? It's the next cigarette.

2. There is absolutely nothing to give up or sacrifice. Cigarettes do absolutely nothing for you. Just like millions of others, you were cynically misled by a manipulated mental model. When I write that there is absolutely nothing to sacrifice and nothing to give up, I don't mean that the disadvantages of smoking outweigh the advantages, I mean that there are no genuine advantages, *none whatsoever*. It is nothing more than nicotine addiction. The only 'pleasure' is the partial and momentary relief of the suffering caused by the previous cigarette. The only reason that certain cigarettes appear special (after eating, for example) is that you smoke them in what are happy and agreeable moments anyway, irrespective of whether or not you are a smoker. The difference is that if the smoker cannot get his nicotine fix, he becomes irritable and anxious. The only reason that a smoker lights a cigarette is to end the discomfort caused by the previous cigarette. Everything else is mental manipulation.

3. Enjoy your decision: You are taking back control of your life. You are deciding to live a longer, healthier and happier life. Imagine it! More energy, vitality, peace of mind, money, more confidence, courage, better concentration; you will smell better and your skin will be more radiant. You are liberating yourself of years of the nightmarish bondage of drug addiction. There is nothing to feel depressed or deprived about. This is truly a cause for joy and happiness, not just today but for the whole of your life. To never again have to systematically poison yourself with nicotine and the other four thousand toxic chemical compounds in cigarettes. To be free. Wonderful!

Your decision is the following: I will never smoke another cigarette, irrespective of the good times or the bad times that I might have in my life. Not a puff of tobacco ever again. Whatever happens, whatever it might be, I will face it physically and mentally stronger as a non-smoker. I will enjoy my decision and my freedom.

Don't fall into the trap of thinking that you might sometime be able to smoke just one cigarette or an occasional cigarette. *There is no such thing.* There never has been. It was that lie that got you hooked in the first place, that made you an addict. Let us imagine for a moment that you are so bone headed that you believe that it is possible to smoke an occasional cigarette and not get hooked. What would the possibilities be for you?

The first is that you never smoke a cigarette for the rest of your life but believe the illusion, "I could smoke just one" With this attitude you guarantee a life of feeling miserable because you cannot have something that simply doesn't exist. You'll be whining and pining for something that you yourself don't want. Not only is that pointless but also pretty stupid!

The second possibility is that you smoke another cigarette. By doing that, you'll swap feeling miserable for feeling depressed when you realise that you are back to where you were: a nicotine addict, that is a smoker who has to smoke all day every day until you die.

There is a common saying that nothing in life is black and white and that really it is all shades of grey.

Smoking or not smoking is black and white. Smoking is all or nothing. There is no middle ground.

Remember the reason that you read this book in the first place is that you hate being a smoker. Accept it. Accept the reality. It's simply marvellous to be free.

You have made your decision. Once you put out that last cigarette you are free. You are a non-smoker. Think of it as a fact: ***You are a non-smoker***. Not as some future state. Stopping smoking is like any big change in your life. You need time to get used to the new situation. This has nothing to do with your decision; it's just an adjustment period. It is merely the difference between the belief that you are free and confirming that freedom through experience.

27
Now accept your decision

Acceptance, such a simple word for a simple concept and yet it remains the least understood part of being a non-smoker and remaining happy about it for the rest of your life. This misunderstanding of what acceptance means can cause problems not just for stopping smoking but in many other important aspects of life.

The people that I see in the back-up sessions are often there because they don't fully understand what acceptance is. They ask questions like: "But what do I have to do?" "I just cannot stop thinking about it. I'm really trying to accept my decision." They are desperate to know exactly what they have to *do* to accept their decision. The answer is of course nothing. If that sounds paradoxical, let me explain:

One of the principal reasons acceptance feels strange is that all of our lives we are trained to *try*. If we want something, we have to 'work' to get it. "Things don't happen without *effort and discipline*." In order to achieve anything worthwhile you have to *work at it*." Whilst this is clearly true for many of life's projects, for stopping smoking it is the opposite of what you should do. Working hard to accept your decision is like working hard to get to sleep. Utterly futile.

There is a prayer by Reinhold Niebuhr, called the Serenity Prayer. Here is a small part of it:

> *God grant me the serenity*
> *to accept the things I cannot change;*
> *courage to change the things I can;*
> *and the wisdom to know the difference.*

Irrespective of whether or not you happen to believe in God, the sentiments expressed by Reinhold Niebuhr are valid. The fact is we can all change. **Your past is not your future.** Many things can and perhaps should be changed. The drug nicotine will never change, nor the way that it enslaves its users and the horrific damage that it causes. Nor will human nature ever change (at least not on a time scale that will affect you). The big industries involved in the manufacture and promotion of

161

addictive drugs will always put their interests before yours. Most of the organizations and associations that you believe are there to protect you, will always put their interests first. Big industries will always lie and manipulate you to turn a profit. However, none of this will affect you if you *accept* the reality of what smoking (nicotine addiction) is, if you **accept** your decision. To not accept these facts is to wish (pointlessly) that reality were somehow different to what it is. It is this desire, this non-acceptance of reality that can make you vulnerable.

Accept what? Accept that there is nothing to sacrifice and absolutely nothing to give up. Addiction to the drug nicotine is the same as the addiction to any drug. An addictive drug creates the need for itself. An addictive drug creates a sense of emptiness, of something 'missing'. You then mistakenly use more of that same drug to fill the emptiness that the drug itself created, creating a new wave of emptiness. In order to protect you, your body develops tolerance to the drug which means that you need more of it to fill the emptiness created by the last fix. However, as you increase your consumption, so your tolerance increases. Each dose brings less relief and so you feel you need to smoke even more. Very quickly you find yourself in a losing battle. It is a battle that you can never win, only die trying. You soon find yourself smoking ever more just trying to get back to feeling 'normal'. Smoking no longer feels like a choice but an obligation. It really doesn't matter what the drug might be, all addicts end up at this place of fear and slavery, consuming as much of the drug as their bodies can stand, whilst suffering an almost constant state of withdrawal. Put in smoking terms that means that the only genuine reason for which anyone smokes is to try and relieve the withdrawal caused by the previous cigarette *in the attempt to get back to feeling normal... in other words to feel like a non-smoker again.*

There are many drugs to which you can become addicted but nicotine must be one of the most pointless ones. I am in no way advocating drug use but at least with marijuana or alcohol you get (however briefly) an insidious, mind-bending illusion of happiness. With nicotine you just feel anxious and distressed if you cannot use it. These are the facts, the reality. It always was and always will be the reality, no matter how you might wish that things were different. There is nothing to try for, nothing to work at. In the same way as water is wet, you don't have to *try* to make it wet or *work at* it being wet. Water cannot be anything else; it is the nature of water to be wet. It always was and always will be.

Accept that there is no such thing as 'just one cigarette'. There never was and there never will be. Every cigarette that you have ever smoked was the direct result of that 'just one' experimental cigarette all those years ago. Since then you've tried pretending that there was no problem. You've tried 'giving up', mistakenly believing that there was something to give up. You've tried to smoke less; you've changed what it is that you smoke; you've tried in countless ways to *control* it. Did you succeed? Were you happy with the result? Of course not, that's why you're reading this book. The idea of just one cigarette is an illusion, it always was and it always will be. What exists is simply the life of a smoker, an addict to nicotine, a slave to the tobacco industry. To wonder if you can smoke just one cigarette is like wondering if you could immerse yourself naked in a bath tub of water and not get wet. You wouldn't waste time wondering about that because you understand and accept that water is wet, always was and always will be.

You never decided to become a smoker. Like millions of others you were cynically and criminally manipulated into believing that you were experimenting with one cigarette.

Ask yourself, if you knew back then what you know now, would you have ever smoked that first cigarette? Of course not!

Could anything be more straightforward? There are few, if any, decisions that you have taken or will ever take in your life that could be so unambiguously correct. You will know with complete and total security, not only when you take your decision but for the rest of your life, that your decision to stop smoking is, was and always will be the correct one. That is a cause for celebration! Right from the first moment and for the whole of your life! Ask yourself exactly how many of the decisions that you have taken in your personal life have been so clear? For most people there are few or no decisions that have these characteristics. Most decisions carry with them a grain of doubt. What might have seemed like a great decision at the time, we later realize wasn't so good; we would have acted differently if we knew what we know now. Other times we take a decision and in the moment we take it we are unsure whether or not it is the correct one, or perhaps feel that we really have no choice in the matter. Later in life we come to realize that it was the best decision that we could have taken. Your decision to stop smoking is one of the very few decisions that you will ever take and know with complete security – not only in the moment that you take it but also for the rest of your life – that it was, is, and always will be the correct decision. You know it in your bones!

People in general and smokers (especially where stopping smoking is concerned) easily confuse fear with excitement. Fear and excitement

163

produce very similar sensations in the body. Clients experience swings in emotions throughout the session: one moment they are confident and relaxed and the next, nervous and fearful. When we set about exploring their feelings, we discover that a large part of what they believe to be fear is in fact excitement. We are all of us different; some of us are more inclined to feel nervous excitement. Nervous excitement is fine and not surprising, given the wonderful change that stopping smoking and recovering your life represents. You, like most smokers, have probably spent most, if not all of your adult life smoking, a slave to the tobacco industry. Stopping, although marvellous and one of the best decisions in your life, feels like a step into the unknown. Accept whatever feeling you might have. It's temporary and has no bearing on your decision.

Acceptance isn't just 'resigning yourself to your fate'. It is a form of precision thinking. It is first *understanding* that there is nothing to sacrifice. Then *accepting* reality as it is: that there is nothing to give up and no such thing as an occasional, special or 'just the one cigarette'. Then *implementing* the correct steps, ie. stop smoking — a bit obvious really; shutting the door on that part of your life; leaving it behind with the same relief that you experience when you wake up from a bad dream and feel happy that you've got your life back. The only alternative for those who don't accept reality is to put yourself through self-inflicted suffering, that is to say, to pine and whine. In other words, pining for something that doesn't exist (just one cigarette), then whining because you cannot have something that you hope never to have again (the life of a smoker, a nicotine addict — which after all, is all that there ever was or can be).

There are many things that we can change. The nature of nicotine is not one of them. Nicotine is an addictive drug; its only effect is to make you an addict, condemn you to a life of fear and slavery. Accept it!

To accept reality is deeply relaxing.

So much suffering in life is caused by not accepting reality. You have probably experienced the painful lesson of non-acceptance and the relief that acceptance can bring in other areas of your life. For example, perhaps you've tried to keep alive an abusive, damaging or difficult relationship, hoping against hope that things will somehow change. The suffering in these situations is enormous. One day you accept that it's simply not going to happen, that the relationship is going nowhere. Nervously, but with resolve you take the brave step of facing up to the reality and end the relationship. Later in life you look back with a sense of relief and you probably wonder what it was you ever saw in the relationship and why it took you so long to free yourself!

Why did you start smoking again?

Perhaps like me, you learnt that the best way to handle an injection is to simply relax and accept it. The alternative (something that I did for years) – fighting, bracing myself, tensing myself up (my buttocks in particular) – quickly turned a minor discomfort into torture. Perhaps you have fought the need to use reading glasses, finally accepting that you do sometimes need them, then discovering the pleasure of being able to read quickly and clearly once again. The relief in all of these situations comes when instead of fighting reality, you accept it.

It is the absurd, tragic and futile hope that reality will somehow change or the desire that reality were somehow different that can cause problems. Understand and accept what nicotine is and that what it does to you will never change. Think, isn't it truly a relief to both know and accept that?

You are enough. How could you be anything else? You are complete just as you are. It is one of the characteristics of addiction to make you feel that you won't be enough, that you won't be 'you' without nicotine. That's just the nicotine parasite talking. **You are enough!** Remember, **you are enough. Accept it!**

Geoffrey Molloy

28

And now what?

Congratulations on your decision. *You are free from the moment you take your decision.* However, during the next few days – normally about three (it could be as little as two or as long as five), your body will continue to metabolise and eliminate nicotine. We are talking about the physical withdrawal symptoms. I'm not talking about dramas, bad temper, going up the wall. It is simply the physical sensation of your body eliminating nicotine, nothing more! If you become aware of the withdrawal during the next days, you will probably notice a slightly empty, insecure feeling around about your solar plexus. You will probably recognise it as the thought, "I want a cigarette." Now pay attention. Stop calling the feeling, "I want a cigarette". That's how the scumbags in the tobacco industry and their wicked helpers the PR industry got you hooked. Instead, see it for what it really is: just your body eliminating the drug nicotine for once and for all. Instead of thinking, "I want to smoke a cigarette but I can't have one," think, "This is just my body eliminating the last remnants of nicotine. This is what smokers suffer all their lives. It's precisely this feeling which causes the fear, the lies, the disease and the suffering. It is this feeling which keeps them smoking. But I am a non-smoker and I'll soon be free of this feeling, of my body eliminating nicotine. Marvellous! Wonderful!"

By reading and understanding this book you have freed yourself of the parasitic idea, the manipulated mental map, the nicotine scam, the scam that conned you into introducing the nicotine parasite into your body with that first cigarette, the very parasite that has had the control all of your smoking life since then. Many clients have commented that for them it was enjoyable, even very enjoyable, to focus their attention on the marvellous feeling of finally killing that parasite that infected and controlled them all of their smoking lives. When they became aware of the empty feeling, they said things like, "Die you bastard! I'm free!" Now if you want to do that, do so, but never out loud in public! See it as one client explained to me, "I've finally got back control of my life. I've got my life back." "If the SOB parasite doesn't like the new situation, tough luck. He can shout, he can scream, he can do whatever he wants, I don't

167

care because he has no power and soon he'll be dead! I have the reins now. I have control once again of my life. Never again will this parasite make me spend a fortune to systematically poison myself. I am free. Never to be abused again."

You are free, but for some time you will absent-mindedly exhibit some of the habitual, unconscious actions of a smoker. Remember, this doesn't mean that you want a cigarette; it just means that you need time to adapt. You'll find yourself distractedly patting your pockets or opening your handbag, looking for your cigarettes and lighter and then realize that you no longer smoke. This is certain to happen when you are in a social situation, happily chatting and drinking when someone offers you a cigarette. Without thinking you move your hand to take one. As you do so you suddenly remember that you don't smoke. *This will happen*, but don't worry, it is a great sign; it means that you had forgotten about smoking. When this happens, use the moment to enjoy your decision: "Brilliant, I don't have to smoke anymore, I am free."

Count on the fact that you will dream that you have smoked but this is all that it is, a dream. Do not fall into the trap of seeing deeper meanings. You smoked thousands of cigarettes, so of course you will dream of them. Enjoy the relief when you wake up and realise that you are a non-smoker.

I would like now to talk about some of the most typical situations you will find yourself in after stopping smoking and how to deal with them. These situations are so common that I refer to them as syndromes.

Pesky friends and colleagues

You will find that some of the more bothersome ones will pester you constantly, perhaps asking you several times a day, "Still not smoking?" "Don't you miss them?" "Go on, tell the truth. I bet you've had a crafty one." The solution to this is to give them a nice, big smile and tell them that you are free and absolutely delighted to be free. Let them have and enjoy their fantasy. Don't get angry or irritated. Just smile and say, "I'm free and delighted to be free."

The next category – "pesky smokers". You may well find yourself with a friend or acquaintance that knows that you stopped smoking but keeps trying to tempt you with a cigarette: "C'mon! don't be boring, just the one. What harm can it do?" They may even tell you that you have turned into a horrible non-smoker. There is a wonderful saying in Spanish: 'Mal de muchos, consuelo de tontos'. The loose translation is that with regard to things we do that do us little good, it is foolish to console oneself with the fact that many others do them too. However you look at it, smoking is stupid. But whilst the smoker is surrounded by other smokers, he doesn't feel so stupid. The complicity of his smoking companions helps him feel not so stupid. When he sees you, not only as a non-smoker but delighted with it, he will probably experience a mixture of stupidity, hope and anger. Hope, because if you can get free he realises in some part of his heart that he too must be able to do it. Anger because you've abandoned the 'gang'. He is worried that he won't be able to smoke in front of you. It's going to be difficult for him to justify his own smoking and that's why he probably feels a bit stupid. Whatever you do, don't give the smoker a lecture, or a mini stop-smoking session, or tell him off. Give him a smile and tell him that you are free and very happy to be free; that if he wants to smoke, you don't mind a bit: "Please smoke if you want to, I'm a non-smoker and happy to be so." This is the most useful posture for both you and the smoker. You will have the pleasure of seeing a smoker who, just by being around you, will realise that he can free herself.

Now we come to the worst category of all: Family. They know us, have probably seen many failed attempts to stop smoking and no longer believe us when we say that we have stopped smoking. It certainly was my case. People will not always behave as you think they should, nor do they have any obligation to do so. Once again the best response is to smile and tell them that you are free and happy to be free. Enjoy all of these moments; they form part of your freedom.

Finally, remember that the tobacco industry and the people who run it are both cold-blooded and evil. They are helped by the PR/communications industry. Between them they continue to invest thousands of millions of dollars every year to get children hooked and to keep them hooked throughout their adult lives. They don't care how much misery and suffering they cause. They don't care that they take the best years of your life or if you have to die a horrible death, so long as they can make a profit.

Remember whatever they say, whatever you hear:

There is nothing to sacrifice or give up. There never was.

There is no such thing as just one cigarette, just the life of a smoker.

Return to health.

Now that you've stopped smoking, your body will start a process of elimination. Apart from the nicotine, you have spent years systematically poisoning yourself, stressing your immune system with many different toxic compounds. This has now ended.

You have spent years with your body in a pathological state. You now begin the path to full health and wellbeing.

No one suffers all of these symptoms but I list here some of the most common ones. Remember, nothing bad can happen to you because you have stopped smoking. The return to health and the elimination happen not because you've stopped smoking but because *you started in the first place*:

Slightly woolly feeling in the head: This normally lasts a couple of days and is due primarily, to an increase of oxygen in your blood-stream.

A light 'pins and needles' feeling in your fingers and toes: caused by blood flow returning to your extremities.

Cough and an itchy or tickly feeling in the throat: Whilst we smoke we tend to see a cough, particularly a smoker's cough, as an illness, something to be avoided at all costs. A cough is not an illness but a mechanism to eject contamination from your lungs. One of the commonest symptoms on the journey back to health is a cough. It is a good sign.

A cold: Mucus is another way in which the body eliminates unwanted toxins and visitors. When you have a cold the main reason for which you get so snotty is that your body is eliminating the cold virus by producing abundant quantities of mucus.

The elimination process is different for each person. However, the most important aspect is that you accept your path back to full health and energy. To get from A to C you have to pass through B.

Final checklist

1. YOUR DECISION: The decision you have just taken is the correct one. Accept it.

2. THERE IS NO SACRIFICE: You are not sacrificing anything. Accept that you do not enjoy smoking, that you never did and that you never will. The idea that the cigarette helps you or that it is a pleasure is an illusion. There is nothing to give up.

3. SUBSTITUTES: The rotten thing about substitutes is that they perpetuate the falsehood that you are making a sacrifice. Did you need a substitute when you last got over the flu? Of course not! You don't need a substitute.

4. NOT A SINGLE PUFF: You cannot smoke a single cigarette, cigar or anything that contains nicotine. By this I don't mean smoking one cigarette is prohibited or that you shouldn't. What I am saying is that there never was or ever will be such a thing a one puff o one cigarette, just the suffering of the life of a smoker.

5. BACK TO NORMAL: It's likely that you have forgotten how it feels to be a non-smoking adult. It may be something that you have never experienced. If you ride a bike or drive a car after having not done so for many years, then you will need some time to get used to it again. Accept and enjoy your freedom and all the new feelings that this might bring.

6. YOUR ATTITUDE: If you feel like 'something is missing' or if you find yourself thinking, "I want a cigarette," don't waste time thinking, "I want a cigarette but I can't or I shouldn't smoke." Simply think, "This is not a very agreeable feeling. Non-smokers do not suffer this feeling. Soon it will disappear – for good! How wonderful, I am a non-smoker!" Remember, any discomfort you may feel is not because you have stopped smoking, but because you started smoking

7. DO NOT ENVY SMOKERS: If you happen to see a smoker lighting a cigarette and start envying him, remember, he is not having a good time because he is smoking. It's just that if he wasn't allowed to smoke, he would feel depressed and irritable. Get it clearly into your mind that all smokers, either secretly or openly will be envying *you* because all smokers would like to be like *you*, a non-smoker!

8. THROW AWAY ALL YOUR CIGARETTES: Throw away any cigarettes you might have at home, work or any other place for that matter. You are a non-smoker. Non-smokers do not need to have

cigarettes to hand. See it as yet another marvellous opportunity to strengthen your decision.

If you feel you would like to know more about our sessions or skype video support, please get in touch with us:

geoffrey@esfacilsisabescomo.es
*T** 34 942 830399*

Why did you start smoking again?

References

Reference 1: Ineffectiveness of stop-smoking pharmaceuticals
It has been known since April 1993 that nearly 100% of people who use the nicotine patch for a second time start smoking again within 6 months:
http://www.ncbi.nlm.nih.gov/entrez/query.cgi?md=Retrieve&db=PubMed&List_uids=8485431&dopt_Abstract

In November 2003 the results were announced of a study which showed that 36,6% of people who use nicotine gum to stop smoking end up addicted to the gum:
http://tc.bmjjournals.com/cg/reprint/12/3/310

(An Australian study published in May 2006 in 'Addictive Behaviours' showed that the smoker who stops smoking *without* nicotine replacement therapy or other farmaceuticals has *double* the probability of stopping. The study analysed the data collected by 1000 GPs throughout 2002 and 2003:www.nchi.nlm.nih.gov/entrez/query.fcgi?cmd=Retrieve&db=PbMed&dopt=Citation&list_uids=16137834

In September another study published in JAMA (Journal of the American Medical Association) concluded that nicotine substitutes do not increase the success rate in stopping smoking amongst Californian smokers:
http://jama.ama-assn.org/cgi/content/abstract/288/10/1260

Other studies with similar conclusions:
http://content.healthaffairs.org/cgi/content/abstract/21/6/12
http://www.ncbi.nlm.nih.gov/entrez/query.fcgi?cmd=Retrieve&db=pubmed&adopt=Abstract&list_uids=15066370
http://wwwnlho.org.uk/viewResource.aspx?id=7687

The pharmaceutical industry has argued that their studies do show the effectiveness of these pharmaceuticals. The following meta-analysis of such studies point out the manipulation of such studies:
http://whyquit.com/studies/NRT_Binding_Failures.pdf
http://www.forces-nl.org/dowload/DarEtter.pdf

Reference 2: FDA Safety warnings for Chamtix and Zyban, These drugs can cause permanent damage, or death.

Associated Press New York: updated 7/1/2009 7:25:59 PM ET

www.msnbc.msn.com/id/31685329/ns/health-addictions/t/chantix-zyban-must-carry-depression-warning/

The Food and Drug Administration will require two smoking-cessation drugs, Chantix and Zyban, to carry the agency's strongest safety warning over side effects including depression and suicidal thoughts.

The new requirement, called a "Black Box" warning, is based on reports of people experiencing unusual changes in behavior, becoming depressed, or having suicidal thoughts while taking the drugs.

The antidepressant Wellbutrin, which has the same active ingredient as GlaxoSmithKline PLC's Zyban, already carries such a warning.

The FDA is also requiring an additional study on Chantix and Zyban to determine the extent of the side effects. Pfizer Inc., which makes Chantix, said it is still discussing the potential study design with the FDA. The study could include patients with and without psychiatric conditions to determine the true incidence rate of psychological side effects, Pfizer officials said.

Pfizer had already updated its labeling following the beginning of an FDA investigation into the potential side effects in 2007. That investigation was sparked by several reports of psychiatric problems in patients. Despite the new, stricter warnings, the FDA said consumers and doctors still have to weigh the benefit versus the risks when taking the drug.

"The risk of serious adverse events while taking these products must be weighed against the significant health benefits of quitting smoking," said Dr. Janet Woodcock, director of the FDA's Center for Drug Evaluation and Research. "Smoking is the leading cause of preventable disease, disability, and death in the United States and we know these products are effective aids in helping people quit." *(What is not stated here is that numerous studies show that in spite of the very real risks associated with this drug, there is no improvement in stopping smoking at one year when compared to stopping smoking cold turkey- that is to say without any method or medication.)*

Last fall, the FDA also began looking into scores of patient reports about blackouts and injuries while taking Chantix. The Federal Aviation Administration later banned use of Chantix by pilots and air traffic controllers. The drug's label also warns that patients may be too impaired to drive or operate heavy machinery.

Chantix was approved in 2006. Sales reached $846 million in 2008.

"The labeling update underscores the important role of health care providers in treating smokers attempting to quit and provides specific information about Chantix and instructions that physicians and patients should follow closely," said Dr. Briggs W. Morrison, senior vice president of the primary care development group at Pfizer.

I include here an extract of an article written by John R. Polito of the non-profit organisation Whyquit.

http://whyquit.com/whyquit/LinksCAids.html

Link to ISMP report:
http://www.pdfdownload.org/pdf2html/view_online.php?url=http%3A%2F%2Fwhyquit.com%2Fchantix%2FQuarterWatch%25202010q3%2520final.pdf

Further links can be found at the web page address above.

According to a *just released report* by The Institute for Safe Medication Practices (ISMP), a non-profit medication watchdog, "In the first quarter of 2008, varenicline accounted for more reports of serious injury than the 10 best selling brand name prescription drugs combined."

The report indicates that the U.S. Food and Drug Administration (FDA) received serious adverse event reports on 773 different drugs during the 1st quarter of 2008. Chantix again topped the list. During the 1st quarter there were 1,001 new reports of serious injuries among varenicline users, including 50 additional deaths. By comparison, varenicline users accounted for 998 serious injury reports and 78 deaths during the 4th quarter of 2007.

A Pfizer smoking cessation study published in *February 2008* compared 10 weeks of nicotine patch use to 12 weeks of varenicline use. Even after Pfizer gifted varenicline a two-week treatment advantage, varenicline failed to prove superior in 7-day point prevalence findings. Participants were asked at both 6 months and 1 year whether or not they had smoked a cigarette in the past 7 days. Pfizer's researchers, which included four Pfizer employees, were forced to report that there "were no significant differences" between nicotine patch and Chantix smoking abstinence rates at either 6 months or a year.

According to the ISMP report, varenicline again recorded the highest number of suicide/self-harm events of any medication with 226. The combined total for the next two closest drugs reporting suicide attempts was 22% less (oxycodone with 89 reports and acetaminophen with 87).

The report also flags additional kinds of side effects, including serious accidental injuries. It highlights traffic accidents and concerns that varenicline induced seizures, disturbances in vision, panic attacks or impaired judgment may be playing a role.

It encourages further investigation of possible varenicline links to diabetes, potentially life-threatening interruption of the heart rhythm, heart attacks, strokes, and moderate to severe allergic reactions.

The ISMP's earlier May 2008 report raised concerns about potential alertness and motor control related accidents among transportation industry workers using varenicline. In response, the Federal Aviation Administration banned the use of Chantix by airline pilots, the Department of Transportation limited its use among truck drivers, and the Department of Defense prohibited its use by aircraft and missile crews.

Reference 3: Medication and health care leading cause of death: Are doctors and medication really the third leading cause of death in the USA or perhaps even the 1st leading cause of death?

http://www.ncbi.nlm.nih.gov/pubmed/9555760?dopt=Abstract

An original study published by Dr. Starfield, a full professor of public health at one of the most prestigious hospitals in the United States, Johns Hopkins, listed the published research documenting the various causes of deaths that doctors contributed to. Later a Doctor Mercola (www.mercola.com) simply added them all up and compared them to cardiovascular diseases and cancer and came up with the headline, 'Doctors - the number three cause of death in the USA.'

When contacted by Doctor Mercola by e-mail, Dr. Starfield wrote that she disagreed with the headline he had created. She did not feel that doctors were the third leading cause of death, but thought they were the *number one* cause of death because of their failure to inform their patients about the truth of good health.

However, JAMA actually published a study a year earlier that could support that doctors may be the leading cause of death in the United States.

This finding is more of a speculation though, so below are some other studies to support this assertion:

JAMA April 15, 1998; 279(15):1200-5

http://www.ncbi.nlm.nih.gov/pubmed/9555760?dopt=Abstract

- In 1994, an estimated 2,216,000 (1,721,000 to 2,711,000) hospitalized patients had serious adverse drug reactions (ADRs) and 106,000 (76,000 to 137,000) had fatal ADRs, making these reactions between the fourth and sixth leading cause of death.

- Fatal ADRs accounted for 0.32 percent (95 percent confidence interval (CI), 0.23 percent to 0.41 percent) of hospitalized patients.

BMC Nephrology. December 22, 2003

http://www.ncbi.nlm.nih.gov/pubmed/14690549?dopt=Abstract

Why did you start smoking again?

- Medication-related problems (MRP) continue to occur at a high rate in ambulatory hemodialysis (HD) patients.
- Medication-dosing problems (33.5 percent), adverse drug reactions (20.7 percent), and an indication that was not currently being treated (13.5 percent) were the most common MRPs.
- 5,373 medication orders were reviewed and a MRP was identified every 15.2 medication exposures.

Nursing Times. December 9-15, 2003; 99(49):24-5.

http://www.ncbi.nlm.nih.gov/pubmed/14705341?dopt=Abstract

- In 2002, 16,176 adverse drug reaction reports were received, of which 67 percent related to reactions categorized as 'serious.'

Pharmacy World and Science: PWS. December, 2003; 25(6):264-8.

http://www.ncbi.nlm.nih.gov/pubmed/14689814?dopt=Abstract

- Medication administration errors (MAEs) were observed in two departments of a hospital for 20 days.
- The medication administration error rate was 14.9 percent. Dose errors were the most frequent (41 percent) errors, followed by wrong time (26 percent) and wrong rate errors. Ten percent of errors were estimated as potentially life-threatening, 26 percent potentially significant and 64 percent potentially minor.

- Drug-related morbidity and mortality have been estimated to cost more that $136 billion a year in United States. These estimates are higher than the total cost of cardiovascular care or diabetes care in the United States. A major component of these costs is adverse drug reactions (ADE).

American Journal of Medicine August 1, 2000; 109(2):122-30

http://www.ncbi.nlm.nih.gov/pubmed/10967153?dopt=Abstract

- About 0.05 percent of all hospital admissions were certainly or probably drug-related.
- Incidence figures based on death certificates only may seriously underestimate the true incidence of fatal adverse drug reactions.

European J Clinical Pharmacology October 2002; 58(7):479-82

http://www.ncbi.nlm.nih.gov/pubmed/12389071?dopt=Abstract

In one study of 200 patients, ADRs may have contributed to the deaths of two (one percent) patients.
Journal of Clinical Pharmacy and Therapeutics October, 2000; 25(5):355-61

http://www.ncbi.nlm.nih.gov/pubmed/11123487?dopt=Abstract

- In a survey of over 28,000 patients, ADRs were considered to be the cause of 3.4 percent of hospital admissions. Of these, 187 ADRs were coded as severe. Gastrointestinal complaints (19 percent) represented the most common events, followed by metabolic and hemorrhagic complications (nine percent). The drugs most frequently responsible for these ADRs were diuretics, calcium channel blockers, nonsteroidal antiinflammatory drugs and digoxin.

J American Geriatric Society, December, 2002; 50(12):1962-8

http://www.ncbi.nlm.nih.gov/pubmed/12473007?dopt=Abstract

Adverse drug reactions as cause of hospital admissions

Reference 4: WHO Tobacco Report

WHO Fact sheet N°339
July 2011
Key facts
http://www.who.int/topics/tobacco/en/

* Tobacco kills up to half of its users.

* Tobacco kills nearly six million people each year, of whom more than 5 million are users and ex-users and more than 600 000 are non-smokers exposed to second-hand smoke. Unless urgent action is taken, the annual death toll could rise to more than eight million by 2030.

* Nearly 80% of the world's one billion smokers live in low- and middle-income countries.

* Consumption of tobacco products is increasing globally, though it is decreasing in some high-income and upper middle-income countries.

Leading cause of death, illness and impoverishment

The tobacco epidemic is one of the biggest public health threats the world has ever faced. It kills nearly six million people a year of whom more than 5 million are users and ex-users and more than 600, 000 are non-smokers exposed to second-hand smoke. Approximately one person dies every six seconds due to tobacco and this accounts for one in 10 adult deaths. Up to half of current users will eventually die of a tobacco-related disease.

Why did you start smoking again?

Nearly 80% of the more than one billion smokers worldwide live in low- and middle-income countries, where the burden of tobacco-related illness and death is heaviest.

Tobacco users who die prematurely deprive their families of income, raise the cost of health care and hinder economic development.

In some countries, children from poor households are frequently employed in tobacco farming to provide family income. These children are especially vulnerable to 'green tobacco sickness', which is caused by the nicotine that is absorbed through the skin from the handling of wet tobacco leaves.

Gradual killer

Because there is a lag of several years between when people start using tobacco and when their health suffers, the epidemic of tobacco-related disease and death has just begun.

* Tobacco caused 100 million deaths in the 20th century. If current trends continue, it will cause up to one billion deaths in the 21st century.

* Unchecked, tobacco-related deaths will increase to more than eight million per year by 2030. More than 80% of those deaths will be in low- and middle-income countries.

Surveillance is key.

Good monitoring tracks the extent and character of the tobacco epidemic and indicates how best to tailor policies. Fifty-nine countries, representing almost half of the world's population, have strengthened their monitoring to include recent or representative data for both adults and youths, collecting this data at least every five years. Still, more than 100 countries either lack such data or have no data at all.

Second-hand smoke kills.

Second-hand smoke is the smoke that fills restaurants, offices or other enclosed spaces when people burn tobacco products such as cigarettes, bidis and water pipes. There is no safe level of exposure to second-hand tobacco smoke.

Every person should be able to breathe smoke-free air. Smoke-free laws protect the health of non-smokers, are popular, do not harm business and encourage smokers to quit.1

* Only nearly 11% of people are protected by comprehensive national smoke-free laws.

* The number of people protected from second-hand smoke more than doubled to 739 million in 2010 from 354 million in 2008.

* Of the 100 most populous cities, 22 are smoke free.

* Almost half of children regularly breathe air polluted by tobacco smoke.

* Over 40% of children have at least one smoking parent.

179

* Second-hand smoke causes more than 600,000 premature deaths per year.
* In 2004, children accounted for 28% of the deaths attributable to second-hand smoke.
* There are more than 4000 chemicals in tobacco smoke, of which at least 250 are known to be harmful and more than 50 are known to cause cancer.
* In adults, second-hand smoke causes serious cardiovascular and respiratory diseases, including coronary heart disease and lung cancer. In infants, it causes sudden death. In pregnant women, it causes low birth weight.

Tobacco users need help to quit

Studies show that few people understand the specific health risks of tobacco use. For example, a 2009 survey in China revealed that only 37% of smokers knew that smoking causes coronary heart disease and only 17% knew that it causes stroke.2

Among smokers who are aware of the dangers of tobacco, most want to quit. Counselling and medication can more than double the chance that a smoker who tries to quit will succeed.

* National comprehensive health-care services supporting cessation are available in only 19 countries, representing 14% of the world's population.
* There is no cessation assistance in 28% of low-income countries and 7% of middle-income countries.

Picture warnings work

Hard-hitting anti-tobacco advertisements and graphic pack warnings – especially those that include pictures – reduce the number of children who begin smoking and increase the number of smokers who quit.

Studies carried out after the implementation of pictorial package warnings in Brazil, Canada, Singapore and Thailand consistently show that pictorial warnings significantly increase people's awareness of the harms of tobacco use.

Mass media campaigns can also reduce tobacco consumption, by influencing people to protect non-smokers and convincing youths to stop using tobacco.

* Just 19 countries, representing 15% of the world's population, meet the best practice for pictorial warnings, which includes the warnings in the local language and cover an average of at least half of the front and back of cigarette packs. No low-income country meets this best-practice level.
* Forty-two countries, representing 42% of the world's population, mandate pictorial warnings.
* Graphic warnings can persuade smokers to protect the health of non-smokers by smoking less inside the home and avoiding smoking near children.
* More than 1.9 billion people, representing 28% of the world's population, live in the 23 countries that have implemented at least one strong anti-tobacco mass media campaign within the last two years.

Why did you start smoking again?

Ad bans lower consumption

Bans on tobacco advertising, promotion and sponsorship can reduce tobacco consumption.

   * A comprehensive ban on all tobacco advertising, promotion and sponsorship could decrease tobacco consumption by an average of about 7%, with some countries experiencing a decline in consumption of up to 16%.
   * Only 19 countries, representing 6% of the world's population, have comprehensive national bans on tobacco advertising, promotion and sponsorship.
   * Forty-six per cent of the world's population lives in countries that do not ban free distribution of tobacco products.

Taxes discourage tobacco use.

Tobacco taxes are the most effective way to reduce tobacco use, especially among young people and poor people. A tax increase that increases tobacco prices by 10% decreases tobacco consumption by about 4% in high-income countries and by up to 8% in low- and middle-income countries.

   * Only 27 countries, representing less than 8% of the world's population, have tobacco tax rates greater than 75% of the retail price.
   * In countries with available information, tobacco tax revenues are 154 times higher than spending on tobacco control.

WHO response

WHO is committed to fight the global tobacco epidemic. The WHO Framework Convention on Tobacco Control entered into force in February 2005. Since then, it has become one of the most widely embraced treaties in the history of the United Nations with more than 170 Parties covering 87% of the world's population. The WHO Framework Convention is WHO's most important tobacco control tool and a milestone in the promotion of public health. It is an evidence-based treaty that reaffirms the right of people to the highest standard of health, provides legal dimensions for international health cooperation and sets high standards for compliance.

In 2008, WHO introduced a package of tobacco control measures to further counter the tobacco epidemic and to help countries to implement the WHO Framework Convention. Known by their acronym MPOWER, the measures are identified as 'best buys' and 'good buys' in tobacco control. Each measure corresponds to at least one provision of the WHO Framework Convention on Tobacco Control.

The six MPOWER measures are:
    * Monitor tobacco use and prevention policies
    * Protect people from tobacco use
    * Offer help to quit tobacco use
    * Warn about the dangers of tobacco

* Enforce bans on tobacco advertising, promotion and sponsorship
* Raise taxes on tobacco.

For more information contact:
WHO Media centre
Telephone: +41 22 791 2222
E-mail: mediainquiries@who.int
1 Scollo M, Lal A, Hyland A, Glantz S (2003), Review of the quality of studies on the economic effects of smoke-free policies on the hospitality industry, Tobacco Control;12:13–20

For additional reading I recommend:
WHO report on the global tobacco epidemic 2011.
http://www.who.int/tobacco/global_report/2011/en/index.html

Reference 5: How does nicotine affect your body?

US Department of Defense website:
http://www.ucanquit2.org/facts/nicotine.aspx

There are so many dangers associated with using tobacco products that sometimes the harmful effects of nicotine alone get lost in the shuffle. Nicotine adversely affects EVERY major system in the human body. As it builds up from regular use, it can lead to weakened immune function, fatigue, decreased healing time, and long-term diseases including cancer. In fact, nicotine prevents the body from properly disposing of damaged cells, thereby allowing cancer cells to develop.

Whether nicotine comes from smoke, chew, or use of newer e-cigarettes or dissolvable tobacco, nicotine affects each user in the same ways. Let's break down the body and see how nicotine impacts individual parts:

- Brain: Nicotine disrupts normal neurotransmitter activity, causing chemical changes and addiction. Other neurological symptoms caused by nicotine include light-headedness, sleep disturbance, dizziness, and tremors.
- Heart and Arteries: Nicotine increases heart rate and raises blood pressure when it stimulates the release of adrenaline. Short term, this means your body is less efficient when you exercise. It has to work harder getting the blood and oxygen to cells that need it, preventing the body from reaching its maximum potential. Long term, the stress on the heart and arteries can lead to increased risk of heart attack and can even lead to a stroke and/or aneurysm.
- Eyes: Nicotine reduces the ability to see at night by stopping the production of pigments in the eyes specially designed for low-light

182

vision. Adrenaline released by nicotine reduces peripheral vision, and in the end, nicotine accelerates the degeneration of the eyes.

- Metabolism: Nicotine increases calories burned but decreases endurance by wasting energy in the effort. So, while nicotine users may have the energy to sprint down the block, they won't have the maximum lung or heart capacity to get their best score on a PT running test or maybe even to finish the all-night trek with their unit.
- Reproductive System: Nicotine prohibits proper blood circulation and is the number one cause of erectile dysfunction (impotence) for men under 40. Nicotine also increases the risk of infertility and miscarriage. And if babies exposed to nicotine in utero do make it to birth, they tend to have low birth rates, be born prematurely, and have increased risk for lung problems.
- Bones: When used over time, nicotine alters cellular structures and has been found to increase risk for fractures while contributing long-term to the development of weakened bones (osteoporosis).

Smokers are at an additional risk because nicotine is present in their lungs. Nicotine causes rapid and shallow respiration, leading to quicker fatigue during exercise. Over time, nicotine permanently damages the cells in the lungs by changing their structure. This leads to increased risk for lung disease, lung cancer, emphysema, pneumonia, and bronchitis.

Reference 6: Collusion between Big Tobacco and Hollywood

Acknowledgements and thanks for original compilation to:
Multicultural Advocates for Social Change On Tobacco
www.mascotcoalition.org

Hollywood Stars Encourage Youngsters to Smoke
Travolta and Stone Smoking Plugs
ABC News (Australia)
Saturday, February 24, 2001

Leading Hollywood actors John Travolta, Leonardo DiCaprio, Sharon Stone and Julia Roberts have been accused of encouraging young people to take up smoking by lighting up on screen. Research published in the British Tobacco Control Journal found United States students aged 10 to 19 whose favourite stars smoked on screen were more likely to smoke than those whose favourite stars never smoked in movies.

More than 630 students from rural schools in New England were surveyed about their smoking habits and their attitudes to smoking for the study, and were asked to name their favourite movie star. The researchers then assessed on-screen smoking by 43 movie stars in films made between 1994 and 1996. They found youths whose favourite stars smoked on screen were far likelier to smoke than their classmates whose favourite actors never smoked, and the more the actor smoked, the more favourably the teen viewed smoking.

Fans of DiCaprio, Stone and Travolta, who each smoked in three or more films, were 16 times likelier to express a favourable opinion about smoking than those who chose 'non-smoking' stars. "Mass media portrayals of smoking among favoured movie stars contribute to adolescent smoking which is, in turn, a causal link in what remains the leading cause of premature death and the number one preventable public health problem in the developed world," the researchers write.

Not Just Hollywood Movies -- TV as well
The Washington Post
Feb 26, 2001
by Ann Landers
Page C09

I recently watched an episode of a TV show I have enjoyed for several months. It is a medical series, well done and very interesting, but I will not watch it again. The reason? During the show, which is fictional, four of the doctors were having a conversation in a medical setting. Two of the doctors were nonchalantly smoking cigarettes.

What you have just described is a subtle form of 'product placement'. Whether or not the brand of the cigarette was shown, it was, nevertheless, a clever endorsement of smoking by someone portraying a medical professional.

This is reprehensible, to put it politely… I hope others who notice this sort of product placement will write to the people who produce and sponsor the show and let them know how they feel about it.

Background Research

A study in the current edition of The Lancet [complete study] has generated a great deal of media coverage. The authors viewed the contents of the top 25 US box-office films for each year of release, from 1988 to 1997, and found: "More than 85% of the films contained tobacco use. Tobacco brands appeared in 70 (28%) films."

The authors also found "there was a striking increase in the type of brand appearance depicted, with actor endorsement increasing from 1% of films before the [1989 voluntary ban on paid product placement by the tobacco industry] to 11% after. Four US cigarette brands accounted for 80% of brand appearances." Finally, the authors find: "The most highly advertised US cigarette brands account for most brand appearances, which suggests an advertising motive to this practice."

By way of modest contrast to the Lancet study, the author of a letter to the editor of the British Medical Journal (BMJ) defends tobacco industry advertising practices, noting that "every manufacturer of a legal product will do everything within the law to encourage use."

Why did you start smoking again?

Marlboro cigarettes accounted for 40% of the brands depicted in films. A recently discovered tobacco industry document illustrates the role Hollywood plays in tobacco marketing and promotion. From Philip Morris files related to the National Smokers' Alliance, this document highlights "Possible Advisory Board Members (including some candidates for spokesperson)" see page 1 & page 2.

New York Times/Reuters
Friday, January 5, 2001
By REUTERS
LONDON (Reuters) –

Hollywood stars who smoke in films encourage young fans to do the same, according to a new U.S. study published on Friday. And despite a ban on tobacco companies paying film-makers to place their products in the movies, there is no sign that the practice is becoming less common, according to the research published in the British medical journal, The Lancet.

Doctors led by James Sargent of the Dartmouth-Hitchcock Medical Center in Lebanon, New Hampshire, looked at the 25 top U.S. box office releases for the years 1988 to 1997 -- 250 movies in total. They found that more than 85 percent of the films featured tobacco use and specific tobacco brands appeared in 28 percent of the movies.

Tobacco brands appeared in almost as many films suitable for adolescent audiences as for adults. Among films suitable for youngsters that featured tobacco brands the researchers singled out Ghostbusters II, Home Alone 2 (Lost in New York), Honey I Shrunk the Kids, Kindergarten Cop, Men in Black, My Best Friend's Wedding, The Nutty Professor and Volcano.

The researchers also compared films produced before the 1989 voluntary ban on paid product placement by the tobacco industry and those made afterwards. Overall, there was no change in the prevalence of tobacco brand appearances as a result of the ban and there was a "striking increase" in endorsement of brands in films by actors.

Before the ban, these actor endorsements occurred in one percent (1%) of films, while after the ban this rose to eleven percent (11%). The study suggested that despite the ban on paid product placement, "the tobacco industry might continue to pay directly or through in-kind payments for placement of its brands in films."

Four U.S. cigarette brands accounted for 80 percent of brand appearances in the movies.

"Tobacco-brand appearances are common in films and are becoming increasingly endorsed by actors," the study said.

"The most highly advertised U.S. cigarette brands account for most brand appearances, which suggests an advertising motive to this practice."

The article printed several pictures from films where actors could be seen endorsing Marlboro cigarettes, including Julia Roberts in My Best Friend's

Wedding. Tobacco-control advocates are concerned about the depiction of tobacco use on screen because of the potential effect it could have on adolescents starting and carrying on smoking," the researchers said. They said that studies had shown "an association between on-screen smoking in an adolescent's favourite movie actor and his or her own smoking behaviour."

Ban Fails to Stop Film Smoking Ads
Cigarettes Still Often Featured in Films
BBC News
Friday, 5 January, 2001

Cigarettes are still prominently displayed in films, despite a voluntary ban on "product placements" a decade ago, say researchers. A study of the top 25 US box office films each year from 1988 to 1997 found the use of actors to promote cigarette brands had increased ten-fold.

The researchers say it is uncertain whether film makers are flouting the ban, or if certain brands are used to add realism to the film. Anti-smoking campaigners in the UK said they believe the tobacco companies were finding ways around the restrictions.

Researchers from Dartmouth Medical School, New Hampshire, looked at how often the brand name, logo or trademark was seen, and how often actors were seen handling or smoking certain brands.

Celluloid smoking

- 85% contained tobacco use
- 28% included tobacco brands
- 32% of films aimed at teenagers included brand placements compared to 35% of those for adult audiences
- They appeared in 20% of children's film
- Actor endorsement increased from 1 - 11% of branch appearance
- Four US brands made up 80% of appearances

There are as many product placements for top tobacco brands after as before the 1990 ban. The researchers say the increasing prevalence of just a few brands suggest they are being actively advertised. The placements reach an international audience, with revenues outside the USA accounting for 49% of the total income for the films studied.

Only one previous study has involved the assessment of tobacco-brand placement. It did not report an increasing trend in tobacco brand use between 1985 and 1995.

Dr James Sargent led the research, which found a quarter of the 250 films studied featured recognizable brands. Marlboro cigarettes accounted for 40% of the brands depicted in films, including My Best Friend's Wedding, Men in Black and Volcano. The appearance of cigarette brands in films, especially when endorsed by actors, is no different from other forms of cigarette advertising.

One in five films aimed at children had some kind of 'brand appearance', including Home Alone 2 starring Macaulay Culkin, and Honey, I Shrunk the Kids. Dr Sargent said, "The appearance of cigarette brands in films, especially when endorsed by actors, is no different from other forms of cigarette advertising."Any country that uses advertising restrictions to control tobacco use should restrict this practice."

Dr Sargent said, "Actor endorsement of a cigarette brand associates a type of person with that brand."As viewers assimilate these attitudes towards tobacco, use becomes more favourable." He said there was concern about the depiction of tobacco use on screen because of the potential effect it could have on teenagers' smoking habits.

Dr Sargent added, "The concern is the same for populations in countries where US tobacco products are heavily marketed, and where people are receptive to the advertising message, for whom films present a seductive, affluent, imaginary world."

Before the 1990 ban, tobacco companies paid tens of thousands of pounds to place their cigarettes in the hands of a film's star. But the code is only voluntary and does not stop films featuring cigarette brands, just payment for endorsements.

'Finger of suspicion': Amanda Sandford, research manager for Action on Smoking and Health (ASH) said, "Although paid product placement of cigarette brands was supposed to have ended in the late 1980s, it looks as though tobacco companies are still using actors to advertise their brands.

Amanda Sandford of ASH: 'Marketing tool'
"Branded products don't just appear by accident - a lot of planning goes into what products appear in films and who will be using them. The finger of suspicion points towards a tobacco industry campaign to get round other marketing restrictions."

She said the presence of tobacco brands in films aimed at children makes a mockery of the tobacco industry's claims that it is not targeting the youth market. The research is published in The Lancet.

Tobacco Firms in Row over Film Ban
The Guardian
Friday, 5 January, 2001

There is widespread coverage of a new report published in The Lancet. The Guardian reports that, 'Hollywood actors are increasingly endorsing cigarette brands in films, leading to allegations by medical researchers that the movie and tobacco industries might be flouting a ban on payments for "product placements" in films. The use of actors to promote the most popular tobacco brands has increased tenfold since the voluntary ban was introduced in the US in 1990.

The Guardian further reports, 'The findings have alarmed anti-smoking groups. Studies have shown that smoking by teenagers is strongly influenced by the use of tobacco by their favourite actor. "Tobacco companies know full well that kids are going to see these films and this is probably a deliberate tactic to target the youth market," said Amanda Sandford, research manager for the charity Action on Smoking and Health.

The researchers, from Dartmouth Medical School in the US, said that several possibilities could explain continued tobacco brand appearance in films, from the tobacco industry continuing to pay directly or through payments in kind, to directors using brand imagery to increase a sense of realism or to convey character traits. However, flouting the payment ban would be consistent with regular violation of the cigarette advertising code by the tobacco industry since its inception in 1964.

The article adds, 'The study looked at the top 25 US box office films for each year from 1988 to 1997. The researchers found that before 1990, 1% of the top US box office films showed actors with a recognizable brand of cigarette on screen. But in the years after the ban, 11% of the films showed actors endorsing a brand.

The four most highly advertised US cigarette brands accounted for the most on-screen appearances, including those in hits such as My Best Friend's Wedding, Men in Black and Volcano. More than a quarter of all 250 films studied featured recognizable tobacco brands, including shots of billboards, shop fronts, logos and packets.

Actors Smoking More in Movies Than Before Ban
Bloomberg News
Thursday, 4 January, 2001

..."I can't tell you as a scientist why we are seeing more actor endorsements but we do know that having a famous person endorse a product is effective," said M. Bridget Ahrens, one of the researchers from Dartmouth's Norris Cotton Cancer Center... "We don't have any proof of how the cigarettes got there -- be it clandestine payments, free samples to a particular set designer, or an actor who just happens to smoke that brand," Ahrens said. "But now that we see it and we know what the effect is, we need to answer the question of why it is there."

... Marlboro is the nation's leading cigarette brand, and that may play a role in its frequent use in films, said Tom Ryan, a spokesman for Philip Morris. "Philip Morris doesn't provide any payment for the placement of any cigarette package or cigarette brand advertisements in movies or on television," for at least the

Why did you start smoking again?

past 10 years, Ryan said. "We routinely decline permission when people in the entertainment industry solicit us for our products or permission to use them."

Adults Smoke More on Screen Than in Life
Eagle-Tribune
Monday, 15 January, 2001

Increasing smoke clouds on the silver screen may mean more kids will be lighting up, say local anti-smoking activists after the release of a new study by Dartmouth Medical School.

"It's dangerous," said Diane Knight, coordinator of the Tobacco Free Network at Community Action in Haverhill. "So many young people go to the movies. That's part of their recreation. .... Even if they don't think they are getting the message (smoking is cool), they are."

One consequence of the frequent smoking in movies may be kids think more people smoke than actually do. Diane Pickles, program director for Health Communities Tobacco Awareness Program, finds most children believe more adults smoke than actually do. Only one in seven Massachusetts adults smokes. She thinks perceptions like that feed into the fact that 1,500 youths under 18 start smoking every day.

Reference 7, Side effects of stop smoking drugs

Zyban (buproprion):

http://depression.about.com/od/bupropion/a/bupropioninfo.htm

also:

http://www.drugs.com/stx/zyban-side_effects.html

Never take bupropion if you are taking another drug used to treat depression called a Monoamine Oxidase Inhibitor (MAOI), or if you have stopped taking a MAOI in the last 14 days. Taking bupropion close in time to a MAOI can result in serious, sometimes fatal, reactions, including:

- High body temperature
- Coma
- Seizures (convulsions)

MAOI drugs include Nardil (phenelzine sulfate), Parnate (tranylcypromine sulfate), Marplan (isocarboxazid) and other brands.

Bupropion can cause seizures. Never take bupropion if you have any of the following because you have a higher chance of having seizures with bupropion:

- A seizure disorder
- Take Zyban or any other medicine containing bupropion
- A current or past eating disorder such as bulimia or anorexia nervosa
- Stop suddenly, the use of alcohol or sedatives, including medicines for anxiety and sleeping problems called benzodiazepines.

What Are The Risks?

- Suicidal Thoughts or Actions: **FDA Alert.**
- Seizures: Bupropion can cause seizures. See "Who should not take bupropion?" You also have a higher chance for seizures with bupropion if you take a higher dose, had a head injury, brain tumour, severe liver disease, abuse alcohol or drugs, or take certain medicines that interact with bupropion. Stop bupropion if you have a seizure and never take it again.
- Possible liver damage.
- Serious allergic reactions: Call your healthcare professional right away if you get a skin rash, hives, chest pain, swelling, or trouble breathing.
- Agitation, anxiety, and trouble sleeping
- Mental problems, including psychosis, confusion and hallucinations.
- Mania: You may become hyperactive, excitable, or elated.
- Weight and appetite change: More people lose weight, than gain it, while taking bupropion.
- High Blood Pressure (hypertension). The chance for high blood pressure is increased if you also use nicotine replacement products to stop smoking.

Other side effects include agitation, dry mouth, trouble sleeping, headache and migraine, nausea and vomiting, constipation, and tremors.

Tell your healthcare professional about all your medical conditions, especially if you have liver, kidney, or heart disease.

Tell your healthcare professional if you are pregnant or plan to become pregnant. Tell your healthcare professional if you are breast-feeding or plan to breast-feed your baby.

Are There Any Interactions With Medicines Or Foods?

Bupropion may interact with medicines other than the ones already mentioned in this information sheet, causing serious side effects. Tell your healthcare professional about all the medicines, vitamins, and herbal supplements you take, especially those used for treating seizures, depression, mental illness, asthma, high blood pressure, or heart problems.

Why did you start smoking again?

Champix (Chantix): Side effects

http://www.drugs.com/sfx/chantix-side effects.html

Nausea occurs commonly in people taking varenicline. Other less common side effects include headache, difficulty sleeping, and abnormal dreams. Rare side effects reported by people taking varenicline compared to placebo include change in taste, vomiting, abdominal pain, flatulence, and constipation. In May 2008, Pfizer updated the safety information associated with Chantix, noting that "some patients have reported changes in behaviour, agitation, depressed mood, suicidal thoughts or actions."

In November 2007, the FDA announced it had received post-marketing reports that patients using Chantix for smoking cessation had experienced several serious symptoms, including suicidal ideation and occasional suicidal behaviour, erratic behavior, and drowsiness. On February 1, 2008 the FDA issued an Alert to further clarify its findings, noting that "it appears increasingly likely that there is an association between Chantix and serious neuropsychiatric symptoms." It is unknown whether the psychiatric symptoms are related to the drug or to nicotine withdrawal symptoms, although not all patients had stopped smoking. The FDA also recommended that health care professionals and patients watch for behavioural and mood changes.[7]

Institute for Safe Medication Practices (ISMP) conducted an analysis of post-marketing adverse effects reports received by the FDA. According to this analysis, in the fourth quarter of 2007 varenicline accounted for more reports of serious side effects than any other drug. Suicidal acts and ideation, psychosis, and hostility or aggression, including homicidal ideation, were the most prominent psychiatric side effects. Multiple reports suggested that varenicline may be related to the loss of glycemic control and new onset of diabetes, heart rhythm disturbances, skin reactions, vision disturbances, seizures, abnormal muscle spasms and other movement disorders. ISMP noted that the reports do not establish causality and only identify potential causes, and concluded that further research and a priority review of the data by the FDA is necessary.[8]

On June 4, 2009, The United States Food and Drug Administration announced it was evaluating varenicline for additional potential side effects, including angioedema, serious skin reactions, visual impairment, and accidental injury. [10]

For experiences with Chantix visit: http://quitchantix.com/chantix-blog/
For other articles and links to studies/news:
http://whyquit.com/pr/082506.html

Reference 8: Do Cigarette Warning Labels Increase Cigarette Sales?

Inhaling Fear, New York Times

By MARTIN LINDSTROM
Published: December 11, 2008
Sydney, Australia

http://www.nytimes.com/2008/12/12/opinion/12lindstrom.html

TEN years ago, in settling the largest civil lawsuit in American history, Big Tobacco agreed to pay the 50 states $246 billion, which they've used in part to finance efforts to prevent smoking. The percentage of American adults who smoke has fallen since then to just over 20 percent from nearly 30 percent, but smoking is still the No. 1 preventable cause of death in the United States, and smoking related health care costs more than $167 billion a year.

To reduce this cost, the incoming Obama administration should abandon one antismoking strategy that isn't working.

A key component of the Food and Drug Administration's approach to smoking prevention is to warn about health dangers: Smoking causes fatal lung cancer; smoking causes emphysema; smoking while pregnant causes birth defects. Compared with warnings issued by other nations, these statements are low-key. From Canada to Thailand, Australia to Brazil, warnings on cigarette packs include vivid images of lung tumors, limbs turned gangrenous by peripheral vascular disease and open sores and deteriorating teeth caused by mouth and throat cancers. In October, Britain became the first European country to require similar gruesome images on packaging.

But such warnings don't work. Worldwide, people continue to inhale 5.7 trillion cigarettes annually — a figure that doesn't even take into account duty-free or black-market cigarettes. According to World Bank projections, the number of smokers is expected to reach 1.6 billion by 2025, from the current 1.3 billion.

A brain-imaging experiment I conducted in 2006 explains why antismoking scare tactics have been so futile. I examined people's brain activity as they reacted to cigarette warning labels by using functional magnetic resonance imaging, a scanning technique that can show how much oxygen and glucose a particular area of the brain uses while it works, allowing us to observe which specific regions are active at any given time.

We tested 32 people (from Britain, China, Germany, Japan and the United States), some of whom were social smokers and some of whom were two-pack-a-day addicts. Most of these subjects reported that cigarette warning labels reduced their craving for a cigarette, but their brains told us a different story.

Each subject lay in the scanner for about an hour while we projected on a small screen a series of cigarette package labels from various countries —

including statements like "smoking kills" and "smoking causes fatal lung cancers." We found that the warnings prompted no blood flow to the amygdala, the part of the brain that registers alarm, or to the part of the cortex that would be involved in any effort to register disapproval.

To the contrary, the warning labels backfired: they stimulated the nucleus accumbens, sometimes called the "craving spot," which lights up on F.M.R.I. whenever a person craves something, whether it's alcohol, drugs, tobacco or gambling.

Further investigation is needed, but our study has already revealed an unintended consequence of antismoking health warnings. They appear to work mainly as a marketing tool to keep smokers smoking.

Barack Obama has said he's been using nicotine gum to fight his own cigarette habit. His new administration can help other smokers quit, too, by eliminating the government scare tactics that only increase people's craving.

Martin Lindstrom is the author of 'Buyology: Truth and Lies About Why We Buy'. A version of this article appeared in print on December 12, 2008, on page A41 of the New York edition.

Do Cigarette Warning Labels Reduce Smoking?
Paradoxical Effects Among Adolescents

Thomas N. Robinson, MD, MPH; Joel D. Killen, PhD
Arch Pediatr Adolesc Med. 1997; 151(3):267-272.
http://archpedi.ama-assn.org/cgi/content/abstract/151/3/267

Abstract:

Objective: To examine the association between adolescents' knowledge of cigarette warning labels and actual smoking behaviour.

Design: Cohort analytic study.

Setting: Four public high schools in northern California.

Subjects: Seventeen hundred forty-seven ninth graders (mean age, 14.9 years). Students from 2 of the schools (n=803) were observed for approximately 3 months.

Main Outcome Measures: Self-reported knowledge of warning labels was assessed at baseline. Self-reports of smoking behavior were completed at baseline and at follow-up.

Results: Greater knowledge of cigarette package warning labels was significantly associated with higher levels of smoking. Knowledge of warning labels on magazine and billboard advertisements did not differ significantly by level of smoking. In the longitudinal sample, greater knowledge of cigarette package warning labels was significantly associated with a subsequent increase in smoking, controlling for the baseline level of smoking, sex, ethnicity, and knowledge of warning labels on cigarette advertisements (odds ratio [OR], 1.22;

95% confidence interval [CI], 1.02-1.46). Knowledge of warning labels on cigarette advertisements was not associated with a significant change in smoking behavior (OR, 1.06; 95% CI, 0.82-1.35).

Conclusions: Sizable proportions of adolescent smokers are not seeing, reading, or remembering cigarette warning labels. In addition, knowledge of warning labels on cigarette packages and advertisements is not associated with reduced smoking. The current warning labels are ineffective among adolescents.

Arch Pediatr Adolesc Med. 1997; 151: 267-272

Warnings on Cigarette Packs May Be Counterproductive

New warning labels will begin to adorn cigarette packs and advertisements. For some smokers, death-related warnings actually increase cigarettes' appeal.

Study by: Journal of Experimental Social Psychology

Link to study:
http://www.sciencedirect.com/science/article/pii/S0022103109002285

Link to article:
http://www.miller-mccune.com/health/cigarette-warnings-counterproductive-3454/

New research suggests that, for a certain set of smokers, allusions to death may actually increase the likelihood they'll light up.

That's the conclusion of a paper published in the *Journal of Experimental Social Psychology*, which questions the effectiveness of anti-smoking campaigns that emphasize mortality threats. The researchers, led by psychologist Jochim Hansen of New York University and the University of Basel, suggest a campaign that dispels the belief smoking makes one cool or attractive could be more effective in getting at least some smokers to quit.

Hansen and his colleagues looked at cigarette pack warnings from the perspective of Terror Management Theory, which was developed in the mid-1980s by psychologists Tom Pyszczynski, Jeff Greenberg and Sheldon Solomon. It contends that our awareness of our own deaths creates the potential for extreme anxiety, which we keep at bay by reaffirming faith in our belief systems (which give our lives a sense of meaning) and maintaining a high level of self-esteem.

Reasonably enough, the researchers assert that for some people, smoking is a facet of their positive self-image. They consider the habit sexy or attractive, or perhaps a proud example of their rebellious spirit.

For those individuals, terror management theory suggests mortality-laced warning labels could be counterproductive. The threat to one's life would

194

presumably result in an urge to pump up one's self-esteem — which, for those individuals, could easily mean a renewed commitment to smoking.

To test this concept, the researchers conducted a study of 39 smokers, ranging in age from 17 to 41. Participants filled out a questionnaire designed to measure the degree to which they base their self-esteem on smoking. They then were presented illustrations of a cigarette pack containing a warning message. Half of them read warnings that spoke of the life-threatening consequences of smoking, such as "Smoking leads to deadly lung cancer." The other half read warnings that did not involve mortality, such as "Smoking makes you unattractive."

Following a 15-minute delay in which participants answered questions unrelated to smoking (so that the warning messages would leave their conscious minds), they answered a final set of questions including "Do you enjoy smoking?" "How important is smoking to you?" and "Are you going to smoke a cigarette directly after this study?"

The researchers found that, among those who associated smoking with self-esteem, the death-related warnings actually led to more positive attitudes toward cigarette use. They concluded the smokers clung more tightly to their habit as "a strategy to buffer against existential fears provoked by death-related warning messages."

On the other hand, for these same people, the non-death-related warnings had a dampening effect on attitudes toward smoking. Warnings that smoking makes one less attractive "may be particularly threatening to people who believe the opposite," they report.

The researchers admit it is impossible to know what percentage of smokers ie their self-esteem to the health-impairing habit. Thus, for the population at large, "it is difficult to predict whether a death-related or a death-unrelated warning message would be more effective," they write.

"Yet one could speculate that certain populations base their self-esteem on smoking to a higher degree than others — for instance, young smokers who want to impress their peers," they add. "If this turns out to be true, a consequence of our findings would be that such populations should be warned against noxious consequences of smoking with death-neutral messages."

So those unfiltered warnings that are on the way may be counterproductive with the group the government is trying hardest to target: young smokers. Like previous research on the Montana Meth Project, the study is a reminder that death threats will capture people's attention, but how they impact behavior is a much more complicated question.

Geoffrey Molloy

Why did you start smoking again?

If you feel that alcohol is having a negative effect on your life then read on… Geoffrey has also helped many people stop drinking alcohol. The second edition of his stop drinking book will be available shortly. Here is what some people have said about this programme:

Hello Geoffrey, I just had to write to you. You know what? I've realized that the important thing about stopping drinking isn't so much the time that you have spent without drinking, which in my opinion is neither here nor there. What for me is the most important thing is just how much I am enjoying my life. I value everything so much more. It seems incredible that I have wasted so much of my life drinking. With each passing day I am ever clearer that drinking is something I will never ever do again. I understand the problem perfectly. The important thing is to understand and accept that there is no such thing as just one drink, in much the same way that you can never unlearn how to ride a bike…haha. I just want to say that I am so happy that I called you that day. I thank God that you got me to see the reality, and take my decision; it is the most important decision that I've taken in my life… I've slimmed down 11 kilos and started running again (15 kilometres). Finally the business is going great. (I know that if had carried on as before then the business would have closed by now, of that I can assure you.)
German

Hello Geoffrey, I write because I wanted to say thanks and to let you know that I feel very well and happy. I feel especially happy as since I stopped drinking with you I've not only been through stressful situations but also many social ones (the situations that I worried most about). I never believed that I would feel so strong against the social pressure exerted by my drinking friends: "You've got to be mad to stop drinking and join those boring non-drinkers etc. etc. but my decision has made me feel very strong and more secure in other aspects of my life, knowing that I am now able to face life's problems with a smile on my lips. A big hug
Concha

Geoffrey, You are my saviour! I drank red wine every day of my life since I was very young (for about 35 years or so). I felt as if I could not survive or face life without my ritual of red wine before lunch, before supper, weekends etc. I felt that alcohol was a part of me, that simply I wouldn't be "me" without a drink in my hand. But there was another part of me that felt terrible being a slave to this absurd need, especially since my health was deteriorating noticeably. One day a friend told me about you. I got in touch and my life changed forever. After talking with you for about six hours I took my decision to never drink again, and that is exactly what has happened. But best of all, right from the very beginning I did it without any suffering, and without craving, without missing it.

197

Geoffrey Molloy

I am finally, after so many years, free of that horrible addiction thanks to your excellent work. A thousand thanks
Rosa

When, as a teenager, I started to drink, I really didn't give it much thought. I drank socially and thought that drinking, even in excess, was normal. I had no idea that I was falling into an abyss. In my twenties, I started drinking not just socially but to help me relax. I married 8 years ago. Much of that time was conditioned by the terrible temper and harsh words that normally came out after a few glasses of red wine. Our marriage had become a place where we simply went to hurt each other. My addiction also made me impatient with my daughters, and for no good reason they found themselves at the receiving end of my anger. As much as I tried to deny it I could see that I had a serious problem, but the only system I was aware of for stopping drinking was Alcoholics Anonymous. I just didn't see myself as one of them. I simply didn't believe that I was an incurable alcoholic. I had the good fortune to find Geoffrey's program, which helped me see the reality of alcohol and its subtle and not so subtle effects on those who drink it. I went to one of his sessions and what a surprise to find myself amongst "normal folk". The others in the session were a dentist, a psychologist and a doctor. It was such a relief to not feel strange or different. Thank you Geoffrey for helping me get my life back. This past year since I stopped drinking my marriage though not perfect, is much better, so is my relationship with my children. For the first time in years I feel really good about myself. The only thing that I sometimes regret is that I didn't see and understand the reality of alcohol earlier. Thanks also for seeing the strength in me when I believed that I didn't have any and helping me to do something that I knew I should but never had the courage to do so. Anyone who is in a situation similar to the one that I was in (and I know that there many of you), I encourage you to find the courage to face it. We can all turn our lives around. I write this as to express my thanks and gratitude for so many things, I couldn't think of a better way
Cristina

Hi Geoffrey
Very quickly, two years without drinking alcohol and I feel great. Thank you.
Pedro

Why did you start smoking again?

Geoffrey Molloy

Made in the USA
Charleston, SC
03 January 2012